AF377895

MISSION REDISCOVERED: TRANSFORMING DISCIPLES

A Commentary on the Arusha Call to Discipleship

To the inspiring memory
of the Rev. Robina Winbush
(1957–2019),
co-moderator of Harvesting
Group, WCC Arusha World
Mission Conference 2018.
She died, as she lived,
pursuing the ecumenical vision
of justice and peace.

MISSION REDISCOVERED: TRANSFORMING DISCIPLES

A Commentary on the Arusha Call to Discipleship

Kenneth R. Ross

MISSION REDISCOVERED: TRANSFORMING DISCIPLES
A Commentary on the Arusha Call to Discipleship
Kenneth R. Ross

© 2020 WCC Publications & Globethics.net
Globethics.net, Geneva.
Globethics.net Co-Publications Series.
Director: Prof. Dr Obiora Ike, Executive Director of Globethics.net in Geneva and Professor of Ethics at the Godfrey Okoye University Enugu/Nigeria.
Managing Editor: Dr Ignace Haaz, Globethics.net.

Coordinator Editor WCC Publications: Lyn van Rooyen
Cover and book design: Michael Cagnoni
Photography: Albin Hillert
Print ISBN: 978-2-88931-370-9
Web ISBN: 978-2-88931-369-3

World Council of Churches
150 route de Ferney, P.O. Box 2100
1211 Geneva 2, Switzerland
https://www.oikoumene.org
Email: publications@wcc-coe.org.

Globethics.net International Secretariat
150 route de Ferney
1211 Geneva 2, Switzerland
https://www.globethics.net
Email: publications@globethics.net

WCC Publications is the book publishing programme of the World Council of Churches. Founded in 1948, the WCC promotes Christian unity in faith, witness and service for a just and peaceful world. A global fellowship, the WCC brings together more than 350 Protestant, Orthodox, Anglican and other churches representing more than 580 million Christians in 120 countries and works cooperatively with the Roman Catholic Church. Opinions expressed in WCC Publications are those of the authors.

The electronic version of this book can be downloaded for free from the Globethics.net website: www.globethics.net/publications. The electronic version of this book is licensed under the Creative Commons. Attribution-NonCommercial-NoDerivatives 4.0 International License (CC BY-NC-ND 4.0)

CONTENTS

PREFACE

When the ecumenical movement generates a definitive text, this is invariably the result of discussions with a global range that have been both extensive and intensive. "The Arusha Call to Discipleship" is no exception. A particular task of the World Council of Churches (WCC's) Commission on World Mission and Evangelism (CWME) is to convene, every decade or so, a World Mission Conference to take account of the meaning of the mission to which Christ's followers are called. The ever-changing landscape of both world and church means that this task is never complete. Hence the World Mission Conference convened at Arusha, Tanzania, in March 2018 applied itself to the question of Christian mission as the second decade of the 21st century drew to its close. It generated a text titled "The Arusha Call to Discipleship" (the Call), which attempts to give expression, in brief, to the meaning of mission in our time.

When such a text appears, it deserves a literature. In the case of the Arusha Call, the WCC CWME devoted a full issue of *International Review of Mission* (107.2, 2018) to critical reflections on the text, published a comprehensive report of the conference, and prepared a devotional guide to support the use of the Arusha Call in church life. The commentary offered in this small book aims to complement these early publications by working through the text of the Call systematically, teasing out the intention and meaning of each section.

In preparing the book, I have been able to draw on my experience as an adviser to the WCC CWME. I participated in many of the meetings that prepared for the conference in Arusha. At the event itself, I served as co-moderator of the Harvesting Group, which was responsible for drafting the text of the Call for the consideration of the conference. The same group also prepared the report that accompanied the Call and elaborated on many of its points. I, therefore, write from an "insider" perspective and have intentionally drawn on the body of ecumenical thinking that underlies and informs the Call. At the same time, this commentary is a personal perspective and does not carry any official authority. From my reading, I have selected theological and missiological perspectives that I hope will shed light on the various sections of the Call. I accept full responsibility for any mistakes or shortcomings that the book may contain.

Having made this disclaimer, I hasten to add that the book would not exist without the insight and passion of the members and staff of the WCC CWME. I owe a particular debt of gratitude to the members of its Working Group on Theology for Mission, who offered critical feedback on the text when they met at Kottayam in October 2019, and to the CWME director, the Rev. Dr Risto Jukko, who brought his missional and editorial expertise to the draft. Most of all, I am indebted to the more than 1,000 delegates who came together in Arusha in March 2018 and, together, produced "The Arusha Call to Discipleship."

Kenneth R. Ross
Advent 2019

INTRODUCTION

This small book aims to supply a commentary to assist anyone seeking to understand, and respond to "The Arusha Call to Discipleship" (the Call). The Call is a statement on the meaning of Christian mission in today's context that was issued by the Conference on World Mission and Evangelism held by the World Council of Churches (WCC) in Arusha, Tanzania, in March 2018. The conference was the latest in a sequence of conferences, held roughly every ten years, that have attempted, on an ecumenical basis, to take account of the meaning of the mission to which followers of Jesus Christ are called.[1]

To mention the word "mission" is immediately to step into contested territory. Long gone is the easy complacency that assumed the superior Western world would send missions to benighted and primitive communities in the non-Western world to shape them in its own image. Far from being regarded as heroic pioneers of civilization and progress, the Western missionaries are now more likely to be derided as fanatics who set out to impose their belief system in situations where it was neither needed nor welcome.

At the same time, "mission" is a term that has found new currency in contemporary times. Many organizations will proudly display a mission statement that tells you what they are all about. Users of Apple MacBook computers have a mission control icon on their screen every time they switch on. Clearly, mission has many different shades of meaning and much depends on the context in which it is used.

Christians, too, have been thinking about the meaning of mission. They have realized that they need to honour the missionary endeavour of earlier times while honestly acknowledging its shortcomings. Foremost amongst the latter was the hubris that arose from wrapping faith in assumptions about the superiority of the West. Aware, as we are today, of the economic exploitation and social damage wrought by colonial regimes, as well as the environmental devastation caused by Western-led industrialization, we hope that we will not make the same mistake again.

At the same time, it would be hasty to conclude that the missionary calling was completely mistaken or delusionary. For one thing, there are communities of faith all over the global South that trace their origins to the arrival of Christian missionaries in their area. For another, a century of rethinking has

---

1. Kenneth R. Ross, "Tracing Changing Landscapes and New Conceptions of Mission," in *Ecumenical Missiology: Changing Landscapes and New Conceptions of Mission*, ed. Kenneth R. Ross, Jooseop Keum, Kyriaki Avtzi, and Roderick R. Hewitt (Oxford: Regnum / Geneva: WCC Publications, 2016), 5–146.

set the missionary calling in a very different framework from that which prevailed during the days of Western colonial rule.

This was vividly evident at the Arusha conference in 2018. Its theme was *"Moving in the Spirit: Called to Transforming Discipleship."* It began on a spiritual note, indicating that it would address the spiritual dimension of life. In a market-driven materialistic world, this speaks to all who yearn for nourishment at the spiritual level. It also struck a note of transformation. Who in the context of today's world is not aware of the need for transformation? Whether our analysis is political, economic, ecological, or personal, it is likely to tell us that what is needed is not some gentle amelioration but rather something that is a game-changer. Perhaps the surprise comes with the suggestion of what the game-changer might be: discipleship.

This is not terminology that is in everyday use in the media or in the coffee shop. Somewhere in common memory is the knowledge that Jesus called people to follow him and that those who did were called "disciples." The Arusha conference brought this calling once again to centre-stage, proposing that this might be the driver of the transformation that our world so desperately needs. This book explores this proposal along the lines that were set out at the conference itself.

The conference was the product of a century-long quest to understand the missionary calling. Truth be told, the confidence verging on hubris that was evident when the Western missionary movement gathered in Edinburgh in 1910 did not last long. The First World War, when the so-called civilized nations of Western Europe turned on one another with unprecedented violence, shook the confidence of the missionary movement to its core.

To cut a long story very short, I will identify two key turning points. The first is the realization that "mission" is not primarily about human activity at all. It is first and foremost about the action of God, the "mission of God" (*missio Dei*) in the world, seen in the sending of Jesus Christ and the outpouring of the Holy Spirit. The human dimension is a matter of discerning the action of God and "joining in." This understanding was heralded by the Willingen World Mission Conference in 1952 and gradually came to command a consensus.[2] The second key turning point came at the start of the 21st century with the realization that life itself is at stake. New awareness of the fragile and endangered condition of our natural environment as well as of the prevalence of death-dealing forces in human society opened up a broad canvas for understanding the missionary calling. This found expression in the

---

2. Ross, *"Tracing Changing Landscapes,"* 62–68.

WCC's mission affirmation *Together towards Life*.[3] Jesus' promise of abundant life opens up a wide horizon for the question of the meaning of mission.

It is as this horizon has been explored that the question of discipleship has come into focus in a fresh way. Pope Francis gave a lead when his 2013 encyclical *Evangelii Gaudium* brought together the question of mission with that of discipleship: "Every Christian is a missionary to the extent that he or she has encountered the love of God in Christ Jesus: we no longer say that we are 'disciples' and 'missionaries,' but rather that we are always 'missionary disciples.'"[4] It became apparent that this line of thinking resonated with Christians in many different ecclesial traditions. The crisis of authenticity experienced in the 21st century could be addressed by bringing together two seminal strands of the Christian faith: the missionary mandate and the call to become disciples. Without the Christ-like way of life that is discovered on the path of discipleship, any missionary endeavour is going to lack credibility.

As more than a thousand Christians from every part of the world and from many different ecclesial traditions came together in Arusha in March 2018, they were motivated to explore what it would mean to think of the missionary calling in terms of discipleship. "The Arusha Call to Discipleship" can be read as their discovery of what it means to be "missionary disciples." This brought definition and impetus to an awareness that had been growing in many quarters that a rediscovery of the call to discipleship might be the key to the renewal of mission in our time. Our aim in these pages is to tease out the meaning and intention of the Arusha Call.

The reader is first invited to read the text as a whole, with its 12-fold Call echoing the 12 apostles whom Jesus called and sent, who in turn echo the 12 tribes of Israel and the purposes of God unfolding from ancient times. Then I consider each of the twelve sections in turn, as each articulates a different aspect of the call to discipleship and demonstrates its relevance to urgent contemporary challenges. Aiming to understand each section as deeply as possible, this commentary sketches the background, seeks to discern the intention, expounds the meaning, and concludes with some questions to prompt further reflection.

---

3. Jooseop Keum, ed., *Together towards Life: Mission and Evangelism in Changing Landscapes* (Geneva: WCC Publications, 2013).

4. Pope Francis, *Evangelii Gaudium, Apostolic Exhortation to the Bishops, Clergy, Consecrated Persons and the Lay Faithful on the Proclamation of the Gospel in Today's World*, 24 November (Rome: Vatican Press, 2013), §120, http://w2.vatican.va/ content/dam/francesco/pdf/apost_ exhortations/documents/papa-francesco_ esortazione-ap_20131124_evangelii-gaudium_en.pdf.

THE ARUSHA CALL TO DISCIPLESHIP

WCC Conference
on World Mission and Evangelism
"Moving in the Spirit:
Called to Transforming Discipleship"

The World Council of Churches' Conference on World Mission and Evangelism met in Arusha, Tanzania, from 8–13 March 2018. More than one thousand participants – all of whom are engaged in mission and evangelism – gathered from many different Christian traditions and from every part of the world.

We joyfully celebrated the life-giving movement of the Spirit of God in our time, drawing particular inspiration from African contexts and spiritualities. Through Bible study, common prayer, and worship, and by sharing our stories together, we were encouraged to be witnesses to the reign of God that has come to us through the life, crucifixion, and resurrection of our Lord Jesus Christ.

Despite some glimmers of hope, we had to reckon with death-dealing forces that are shaking the world order and inflicting suffering on many. We observed the shocking accumulation of wealth due to one global financial system, which enriches few and impoverishes many (Isaiah 5:8). This is at the root of many of today's wars, conflicts, ecological devastation, and suffering (1 Timothy 6:10). This global imperial system has made the financial market one of the idols of our time. It has also strengthened cultures of domination and discrimination that continue to marginalize and exclude millions, forcing some among us into conditions of vulnerability and exploitation. We are mindful that people on the margins bear the heaviest burden.

These issues are not new for 2018, but the Holy Spirit continues to move at this time, and urgently calls us as Christian communities to respond with personal and communal conversion, and a transforming discipleship.

Discipleship is both a gift and a calling to be active collaborators with God for the transforming of the world (1 Thessalonians 3:2). In what the church's early theologians called "theosis" or deification, we share God's grace by sharing God's mission. This journey of discipleship leads us to share and live out God's love in Jesus Christ by seeking justice and peace in ways that are different from the world's (John 14:27). Thus, we are responding to Jesus' call to follow him from the margins of our world (Luke 4:16–19).

As disciples of Jesus Christ, both individually and collectively:

We are called by our baptism to transforming discipleship: a Christ-connected way of life in a world where many face despair, rejection, loneliness, and worthlessness.

We are called to worship the one triune God – the God of justice, love, and grace – at a time when many worship the false god of the market system (Luke 16:13).

We are called to proclaim the good news of Jesus Christ – the fullness of life, the repentance and forgiveness of sin, and the promise of eternal life – in word and deed, in a violent world where many are sacrificed to the idols of death (Jeremiah 32:35) and where many have not yet heard the gospel.

We are called to joyfully engage in the ways of the Holy Spirit, who empowers people from the margins with agency, in the search for justice and dignity (Acts 1:8; 4:31).

We are called to discern the word of God in a world that communicates many contradictory, false, and confusing messages.

We are called to care for God's creation, and to be in solidarity with nations severely affected by climate change in the face of a ruthless human-centred exploitation of the environment for consumerism and greed.

We are called as disciples to belong together in just and inclusive communities, in our quest for unity and on our ecumenical journey, in a world that is based upon marginalization and exclusion.

We are called to be faithful witnesses of God's transforming love in dialogue with people of other faiths in a world where the politicization of religious identities often causes conflict.

We are called to be formed as servant leaders who demonstrate the way of Christ in a world that privileges power, wealth, and the culture of money (Luke 22:25–27).

We are called to break down walls and seek justice with people who are dispossessed and displaced from their lands – including migrants, refugees, and asylum seekers – and to resist new frontiers and borders that separate and kill (Isaiah 58:6–8).

We are called to follow the way of the cross, which challenges elitism, privilege, and personal and structural power (Luke 9:23).

We are called to live in the light of the resurrection, which offers hope-filled possibilities for transformation.

This is a call to transforming discipleship.

This is not a call that we can answer in our own strength, so the call becomes, in the end, a call to prayer:

> *Loving God, we thank you for the gift of life in all its diversity and beauty.*
>
> *Lord Jesus Christ, crucified and risen, we praise you that you came to find the lost, to free the oppressed, to heal the sick, and to convert the self-centred.*
>
> *Holy Spirit, we rejoice that you breathe in the life of the world and are poured out into our hearts. As we live in the Spirit, may we also walk in the Spirit.*
>
> *Grant us faith and courage to deny ourselves, take up our cross and follow Jesus: becoming pilgrims of justice and peace in our time. For the blessing of your people, the sustaining of the earth, and the glory of your name.*
>
> *Through Christ our Lord.*
>
> *Amen.*

1. A CHRIST-CONNECTED WAY OF LIFE

We are called by our baptism to transforming discipleship: a Christ-connected way of life in a world where many face despair, rejection, loneliness, and worthlessness.

Called by Our Baptism

Baptism has always played a prominent part in the Christian faith. As the initiatory rite, it has a constitutive and definitive role. It has not, however, always been the first word to be spoken when it comes to stating the meaning of Christian mission. By directing our attention to our baptism, the Call of the Conference on World Mission and Evangelism in Arusha makes the point that to be a Christian is to have a calling to mission. This challenges the common assumptions that there can be an "ordinary" Christian life that is not oriented to mission and that a missionary calling is something only for exceptional people. On the contrary, to enter into the Christian faith, to embark on the Christian life, is already to be a missionary.

We do not baptize ourselves. Baptism is always something we receive from the hand of another. We are first passive before we can be active. We first receive before we can give. It is a matter of a calling that comes from beyond us. So it is also with discipleship. It is not a project that we conceive by ourselves. As "The Arusha Conference Report" states,

> Discipleship is not something that begins with ourselves: "You did not choose me but I chose you" (John 15:16). It begins with a call that comes from beyond ourselves, the call that comes from our Lord Jesus Christ: "Follow me" (Matt. 4:19). One of the best-known features of Jesus' ministry is that he called certain individuals to follow him, to be his disciples.[5]

Because baptism marks a calling to discipleship, to be a disciple is also to be a missionary. Kirsteen Kim has observed that "the conference integrated

---

5. "The Arusha Conference Report," in *Moving in the Spirit: Report of the World Council of Churches Conference on World Mission and Evangelism*, 8–13 March 2018, Arusha, Tanzania, ed. Risto Jukko and Jooseop Keum (Geneva: WCC Publications, 2019), 5–19, 9.

two categories that have often been separated in theology: disciples and missionaries . . . Making disciples is a participation in the *Missio Dei*, the work of the Trinity for the whole creation."[6] This is something that was memorably captured by the Willingen Conference of the International Missionary Council in 1952, and often quoted by Lesslie Newbigin at a vital stage of the ecumenical movement: "There is no participation in Christ without participation in his mission to the world."[7] As Pope Francis stated in his 2013 encyclical *Evangelii Gaudium*, "In virtue of their baptism, all the members of the People of God have become missionary disciples (cf. Mt 28:19)."[8] By taking baptism as its starting point in setting out the missionary calling, the Arusha Call affirms this perspective.

The opening words of the Arusha Call bring together baptism, calling, and discipleship in an arresting way. They remind us that to speak of baptism is already to point to a profound transformation, as the apostle Paul indicated in his Letter to the Romans: "Or don't you know that all of us who were baptized into Christ Jesus were baptized into his death? We were therefore buried with him through baptism into death in order that, just as Christ was raised from the dead through the glory of the Father, we too may live a new life" (Rom. 6:3–4).

Transforming Discipleship

To be a disciple is to respond to the call of Christ by following him, embarking on a Christ-like way of life. From the perspective of the Arusha conference,

> discipleship is an invitation both to a relationship and to a vocation. A relationship that is humble, vulnerable, and mutual, and finds itself growing in following Christ, in Christ's own ways; in finding God at work in situations of strife and struggle; and in empowering people to resist and transform structures and cultures in the name of the triune God. It is, therefore, a vocation of collaborating with God for the transformation of the world.[9]

---

6. Kirsteen Kim, "Mission after the Arusha Conference on World Mission and Evangelism, 2018," *International Review of Mission* 107:2 (December 2018), 418.

7. Lesslie Newbigin, *The Open Secret: Sketches for a Missionary Theology* (Grand Rapids: Eerdmans, 1978), 1.

8. Pope Francis, *Evangelii Gaudium*, §120.

9. "The Arusha Conference Report," 9.

The conference intended the Arusha Call to mean that, instead of being preoccupied with institutional conformity or with securing power and wealth for ourselves, we will hear anew Christ's call to take the risky path of following him. This will entail both deepening our inward spiritual life and expressing our discipleship in outgoing engagement with the world around us.[10] Discipleship is not primarily for our own spiritual comfort but is rather a matter of being gripped by the transformation God promises in Jesus Christ.

A missionary orientation is, by its very nature, a matter of transformation. It is not content to settle for the status quo but, whatever the situation, it is oriented to its transformation in the direction of the kingdom of God. The Arusha conference sought to recover this ferment of transformation in relation to our calling to be disciples. It imagined how transformation might take effect at three levels.

> First, the very idea of discipleship is transformed. Discipleship is often understood merely in the sense of being in a loving, friendly relationship with Jesus. While this is a profound truth, the discipleship we intend to emphasize is one that is not only a relationship, but is actively engaged in continuing Jesus' mission in the world. … Second, we are called to be disciples who are constantly open to being transformed, individually and communally, in our following of Jesus. Discipleship commits us to embark on a spiritual journey that will constantly challenge us and shape us into people who reflect the Lord Jesus in our actions, words, and attitudes. … Third, we are called to be disciples who are ourselves transforming, and as such we are privileged to join in the mission of the triune God, working together towards life, living out the values of the kingdom of God, and engaging in mission from the margins.[11]

The Arusha conference turned to Orthodox theology to find a comprehensive way of stating the calling to be missionary disciples in the concept of *theosis*, often translated as "deification." "Discipleship," states the Arusha Call, "is both a gift and a calling to be active collaborators with God for the transforming of the world (1 Thessalonians 3:2). In what the church's early theologians called 'theosis' or deification, we share God's grace by sharing God's mission."[12] The transforming quality is not something that comes from ourselves but is something we discover as we follow Jesus. As Stephen Bevans

---

10. See ibid., 9–10.

11. Jooseop Keum, "Foreword," in Jukko and Keum, eds., *Moving in the Spirit*, xix, at xviii.

12. "The Arusha Call to Discipleship," in Jukko and Keum, eds., *Moving in the Spirit*, 2–4, at 2.

puts it in his reflection on the Arusha conference, "Disciples become 'other Christs' and so become transforming missionary disciples."[13]

Times of Despair

The resonance of the Call for transformation arises from shared awareness that there is a reality in need of being transformed. This is captured by four words that graphically describe the situation of many in today's world: despair, rejection, loneliness, and worthlessness.

The direction of world affairs leaves many in despair. It appears that "might is right" and that those who hold political and economic power can act with impunity to secure their own interests, leaving many feeling ever more excluded. The golden rule is that "those who have the gold make the rules." Attempts to create a better world appear to have foundered, hopes are dashed, and all that remains is a sense of powerlessness and despair.

No wonder this can lead to a sense of rejection, as people conclude that there is no meaningful place for them. This is vividly and painfully illustrated by the millions of migrants who have had to flee from their homelands in need of succour and support yet find themselves received with suspicion and hostility. It is the experience also of many young people who find that their society seems to have no viable and fulfilling place for them.[14]

Despite new-found technology giving remarkable new opportunities for connectedness, many people confess to feelings of loneliness. No matter how many Facebook "friends" they may have, they feel painfully alone. Ours has been called the "age of loneliness," as people feel that they face the pressures of life all by themselves.[15]

Sadly, this can lead to a sense of worthlessness as young and old alike feel their lives have no value. Absence of affirmation and lack of a sense of purpose have a demoralising effect, leading many to doubt themselves. Self-harm, abusive behaviour, and shockingly high numbers of people resorting to suicide demonstrate the sobering reality that many have lost a sense of their own worth.

---

13. Stephen Bevans, "Transforming Discipleship and the Future of Mission: Missiological Reflections after the Arusha World Mission Conference," *International Review of Mission* 107:2 (December 2018), 375.

14. See, e.g., Douglas Bourn, "Young People, Identity and Living in a Global Society," *Policy and Practice: A Development Education Review* 7 (Autumn 2008), 48–61.

15. See, e.g., George Monbiot, "The Age of Loneliness Is Killing Us," *The Guardian*, 14 October 2014.

The Arusha conference recognized that "we are living in times when our shared life is volatile, uncertain, fragile and fragmented."[16] It lamented the ascendancy of death-dealing forces: "The nationalism and fundamentalism that foment hatred, the militarism that stokes conflict, the greed that concentrates resources in the hands of the few at the expense of the many, and a new type of colonialism associated with the despotic reach of the culture of money." It highlighted

> issues such as forced migration, disease and its effects on the population, ecological degradation, war and conflict, gender inequalities, exclusion and marginalization, appropriation of land, poverty and unemployment, and a reduction of social welfare and security. These issues are reflected and replicated in all regions of the globe, and they are escalating.[17]

The conference therefore concluded,

> Today's world – where so many face the ravages of climate change, fear of the other, uncontrolled conflicts, hatred and discrimination, violence and displacement, unrelenting poverty and the merciless domination of market forces – is a world that cries out for transformation. There is a need for the kind of authentic discipleship that will offer, and live out, convincing answers to this cry.[18]

A Way of Life

The answer proposed by the Arusha conference to the cry of today's world is not a formula, not a philosophy, not a programme of action. Rather it is a "way of life." Here the first words of the conference title are significant: "*Moving in the Spirit.*" Before anything else, this is a matter of spirituality, a matter of inward vitality and formation. Stephen Bevans highlighted the spiritual quality of the Arusha Call: "as Jesus was shaped and formed by the Holy Spirit (see Luke 4:18–19), so Christian disciples are led and formed by the same Spirit as they stay connected to him."[19]

---

16. "The Arusha Conference Report," 8.

17. Ibid.

18. Ibid.

19. Bevans, "Transforming Discipleship," 364.

The recovery of the spiritual dimension has been a hallmark of 21st-century mission thinking. "Today," concluded a study of this question,

> there is a renewal of the missionary impetus of the churches which is marked by its spiritual character. The outstanding case in point is the worldwide Pentecostal/Charismatic movement which is having extensive missionary impact and is unashamed about its emphasis on the spiritual dimension. It has reminded Christianity of its original character, correcting the over-cerebral and over-institutional form which it took during the modern period when global ascendancy apparently lay with the Western churches.[20]

In adopting the term "Christ-connected," the Arusha conference reflected this spiritual orientation.[21] It invites us to think of Christ in terms of connection, taking us into the spiritual realm.

Wherever this occurs, it functions as motivation for mission, moving people of faith to share the good news of Jesus Christ both within their own communities and by crossing frontiers to take the message to new contexts. The WCC's mission affirmation in *Together towards Life* grounds our understanding of mission in the work of the Holy Spirit in an unprecedented way. "Far from spirituality being an afterthought in missiology, to be considered only after the hard-core strategic and institutional issues have been settled, it emerges today as the beating heart of mission."[22] As Frank Chikane summarized it, "When the Spirit comes, people go out."[23]

The fact that the Arusha conference took place on the continent of Africa, the first such conference to do so for 60 years, may have been another factor fostering the spiritual emphasis. "In the turn it took in its post-Western phase," commented the late Yale-based Gambian scholar Lamin Sanneh,

> charismatic religion was more than a spacey rhapsodic binge, just as its effects went far beyond wild spectacles and heady excitement. The West insisted that worship must be of a God who was intellectualizable, because intellectual veracity was the safeguard against mystification and superstition. Yet for Africans, the call for

---

20. Kenneth R. Ross and Wonsuk Ma, "Conclusion: Spirituality as the Beating Heart of Mission," in *Mission Spirituality and Authentic Discipleship*, ed. Wonsuk Ma and Kenneth R. Ross (Oxford: Regnum, 2013), 225–33, at 232.

21. Observation by Stephen Bevans, World Council of Churches Commission on World Mission and Evangelism meeting, Helsinki, Finland, 16–22 May 2019.

22. Ross and Ma, "Conclusion," 233.

23. Frank Chikane, cited in Wesley Granberg-Michaelson, *Future Faith: Ten Challenges Re-Shaping Christianity in the 21st Century* (Philadelphia: Fortress Press, 2018), 104.

explanation was not equal in its drawing power to the appeal of the living God before whose eternal mystery explanation must exhaust itself in worship. Only the reality of a transformed spiritual life could commune with God, which, in part, was the need that the African charismatic movement existed to meet. The religious experience is about intimacy, connection, trust, discovery, and an ethical life in community and solidarity.[24]

Hence, the spiritual quality of discipleship is, at the same time and in the same movement, the action of mission. As the conference report concludes, "Discipleship commits us to embark on a spiritual journey and to adopt a way of life that reflects the Lord Jesus in our actions, words, and attitudes."[25] This implies, comments Stephen Bevans, "that prayer, contemplation, and practices of worship become more and more understood as essential, constitutive of mission."[26]

Being Christ-Connected

The Arusha conference was conscious that, in many contexts, "discipleship" is not a term in everyday use, and it therefore sought language that might help to explain what it involves. Being "Christ-connected" was a phrase that found resonance – living the whole of our lives in close connection with Jesus Christ. It is not shared ideals or common programmes that unite us but rather our connectedness to Christ, our living Saviour and Lord. As Merlyn Hyde-Riley expressed it at a Bible study at the Arusha conference, "To become a disciple is to follow Jesus. At the heart of discipleship, then, is Christ-connectedness – a disciple is bound to Christ."[27]

Stephen Bevans has sought to unpack what it means to be "Christ-connected":

First . . . Christ-connectedness is a fresh, even startling kind of expression, and somewhat attuned to a digital generation for whom "connectivity" is important. Second, the phrase has a more dynamic, perhaps even tactile resonance, in contradistinction

---

24. Lamin Sanneh, *Disciples of All Nations: Pillars of World Christianity* (New York: Oxford University Press, 2008), 193.

25. "The Arusha Conference Report," 10.

26. Bevans, "Transforming Discipleship," 366.

27. Merlyn Hyde-Riley, "Following Jesus: Becoming Disciples, Mark 6:1–13," in *Called to Transforming Discipleship: Devotions from the World Council of Churches Conference on World Mission and Evangelism*, ed. Risto Jukko, Jooseop Keum, and (Kay) Kyeong-Ah Woo (Geneva: WCC Publications, 2019), 7–14, at 9.

to a more cerebral or spiritual tone that "Christ-centred" might imply. In this regard, it is very Pauline and Johannine. Being Christ-connected calls to mind Paul's images of being clothed with Christ (Gal. 3:27), being members of Christ's body (e.g. Rom. 12, 1 Cor. 12), even becoming a sister or brother of Christ through adoption (e.g. Rom. 8:15). The Johannine images that come to mind are being connected as the branches to the vine (John 15:5), or to the image of "remaining" in Jesus' love (John 15:10). Third, the term has a more relational, even reciprocal feel: we are connected to Christ as disciples, and Christ is connected to us. Discipleship thus takes on a feel of mutuality. We matter to Christ. We are loved. We are special.[28]

The organic relatedness evoked by the term "Christ-connected" was once explained by Lesslie Newbigin in these terms: "The absolute condition of fruit-bearing is that the branch is linked to the vine by the multitude of hidden channels through which the life-giving sap can flow. If this hidden flow should stop, the outward appearance of the branch may remain for a time unchanged. It may still have leaves on it. But there will be no more fruit."[29] These words help mission to find its bearings. It is out of the inward connectedness to Christ that authentic missionary action can arise. Here is the indispensable inner spring of transformation. There are many dimensions of discipleship and many manifestations of mission to be explored, but the journey must begin with the call of Jesus and our decision to follow him.

Questions for Reflection

What kind of transformation is imagined in baptism?

What difference will it make to your life if it is Christ-connected?

Why do many feel rejected, lonely, and worthless in our time?[30]

---

28. Bevans, "Transforming Discipleship," 375.

29. Lesslie Newbigin, *The Good Shepherd: Meditations on Christian Ministry in Today's World* (Grand Rapids: Eerdmans, 1977), 140; cited in William Whitmore, "The Branch Is Linked to the Vine: Personal Discipleship and the Missio Dei," *International Review of Mission* 107:2 (December 2018), 477.

30. These and the questions at the end of each chapter first appeared in Risto Jukko, Jooseop Keum, and (Kay) Kyeong-Ah Woo, eds, *Called to Transforming Discipleship: Devotions from the World Council of Churches Conference on World Mission and Evangelism* (Geneva: WCC Publications, 2019).

2. WORSHIP GOD, NOT MAMMON

We are called to worship the one triune God
– the God of justice, love, and grace –
at a time when many worship the false god
of the market system (Luke 16:13).

Confronting a False God

The decision to follow Jesus is not taken in an uncontested environment. Far from it. The Arusha Call acknowledges that in today's world a competing system calls for our allegiance. It is one where the economy is given a place of supremacy and human life is understood primarily in terms of economic utility and prosperity. While such a system has its origins and perhaps its most uninhibited influence in the West, a primary feature of our contemporary context is the extent to which it has established worldwide hegemony. The deifying of the economy, as Jane Collier and Rafael Esteban observe, "has been carried to the four corners of the globe by the institutions of Western culture – not only by bureaucratic and technocratic organizations, but also by the markets that, thanks to the power of modern communications and the force of modern technology, now form the backbone of the global economic order."[31] At a superficial level, this is seen in the near-universal reach of popular brands of fashion, music, and sports. At a deeper level, this globalization is a matter of the growing domination of the free market in governing human life.

Given the growing inequality and injustice of today's world, it might be expected that there would be a great political movement aiming to put things right. However, as Pope Francis has observed: "Something has happened to our politics… It is out of ideas."[32] Faced with gross injustice on a global scale, we might feel that politics has been eviscerated and rendered impotent. The neoliberal global economic order exercises such hegemony that neither national governments nor international institutions can challenge its injustices and excesses. A powerful economic order has been imposed and all are

---

31. Jane Collier and Rafael Esteban, *From Complicity to Encounter: The Church and the Culture of Economism* (Harrisburg: Trinity Press, 1998), 24.

32. Cited in Paul Vallely, *Pope Francis: Untying the Knots* (London: Bloomsbury, 2013), 29.

expected to comply. This is, in the trenchant words of the Arusha Call, "the false god of the market system."

In a report issued on the occasion of the World Economic Forum at Davos, Switzerland, in January 2017, Oxfam pointed out that the world's eight richest individuals have as much wealth as the 3.6 billion people who make up the poorest half of the world, that since 2015, the richest 1 percent has owned more wealth than the rest of the planet, and that over the last 30 years the growth in the incomes of the bottom 50 percent has been zero, whereas incomes of the top 1 percent have grown 300 percent.[33] The report concluded, "As growth benefits the richest, the rest of society – especially the poorest – suffers. The very design of our economies and the principles of our economics have taken us to this extreme, unsustainable and unjust point. "[34]

Such an analysis is echoed in "The Arusha Conference Report":

> When we analyze the causes of these injustices, we see one economic system producing the gross accumulation of wealth for 1 percent of the world's population. This global imperial system has made the financial market one of the idols of our time and has strengthened cultures of domination and discrimination that continue to marginalize and exclude millions, forcing them into conditions of vulnerability and exploitation. Continual exploitation of God's creation to obtain and maintain this economic system is creating conditions of ecological degradation.[35]

The human community is paying a high price for its subjection to the false god of the market system. Highly destructive social and political trends are being unleashed. An Internet age makes people everywhere aware of the privilege of the elite and the extent of their own exclusion. No wonder that resentment and anger are growing, creating a toxic mix of elite-serving authoritarian government, militarism, militant protest movements, terrorism, and loss of values.

To be disciples of Jesus Christ in the face of such forces of history will involve occupying an exposed, risky, and costly position. As *Together towards Life* trenchantly observes, "This is a global system of mammon that protects the unlimited growth of wealth of only the rich and powerful through endless exploitation. This tower of greed is threatening the whole household of God.

---

33. See *An Economy for the 99%*, Oxfam Briefing Paper, January 2017.

34. Ibid., 1.

35. "The Arusha Conference Report," 8.

The reign of God is in direct opposition to the empire of mammon."[36] To be a disciple of Christ today involves a critical stance in relation to the exclusionary dynamics of the global economy.

The "Letter from Accra," produced by the World Alliance of Reformed Churches in 2004, identified the issues at stake and pointed up the difference between the true God and the false:

- Whereas today's neoliberal economy is exclusive, God's economy is inclusive.

- Whereas the neoliberal economy is an exploitative economy of the poor, God's economy is a protective economy in favour of the poor.

- Whereas in the neoliberal economy the flow of wealth is from the poor to the rich, in God's economy it goes from the rich to the poor.

- Whereas in the neoliberal economy the poor are invisible, in God's economy the vulnerable are before everyone's eyes.

- Whereas the neoliberal economy is based on greed and profit-making, God's economy is based on community and mutual support.

- Whereas the neoliberal economy is based on limitless competition, God's economy is an economy of cooperation.[37]

Challenging Empire

The need for Christians to engage critically and prophetically with poverty and inequality proved to be a point of convergence in the mission statements produced by global Christian bodies in the 2010–13 period. The Lausanne Movement's *Cape Town Commitment* challenges Christians to show love toward the poor and explains that "*Such love for the poor* demands that we not only love mercy and deeds of compassion, but also that we do justice through exposing and opposing all that oppresses and exploits the poor."[38] The WCC's *Together towards Life* suggests, "The policy of unlimited growth through the

---

36. *Together towards Life*, §31.

37. World Alliance of Reformed Churches, *Letter from Accra* (Geneva: World Alliance of Reformed Churches, 2004), 36–37.

38. *The Cape Town Commitment: A Confession of Faith and a Call to Action* (Lausanne Movement, 2011), §I 7, www.lausanne.org/content/ctc/ctcommitment.

domination of the global free market is an ideology that claims to be without alternative, demanding an endless flow of sacrifices from the poor and from nature."[39] Pope Francis' *Evangelii Gaudium* raises the same concern: "While the earnings of a minority are growing exponentially, so too is the gap separating the majority from the prosperity enjoyed by those happy few. This imbalance is the result of ideologies which defend the absolute autonomy of the marketplace and financial speculation."[40]

Likewise, the WCC's *Together towards Life* is perhaps at its most uncompromising when confronting the domination of the global free market. The mission affirmation offers a thundering prophetic "no" to a central tenet of late modernity – its claim of supremacy for the global free market. For those who are troubled by the acute inequality and injustice found in today's context, for those who want to believe that "another world is possible," *Together towards Life* is on their wavelength and meets their concerns.

The thinking about mission in the early years of the 21st century has been marked by a growing sense that behind current economic and political trends lies a god-like system making absolute claims and demanding to be worshiped. In his opening address to the Arusha conference, the moderator of the WCC's Commission on World Mission and Evangelism, Metropolitan Geevarghese Coorilos, employed directly imperial language: "There are new incarnations of Caesar. There are new avatars of Herod. There are new emperors. This is a new imperial era where numerous 'little empires' are being created within the orbit of a 'mega empire' that is working in hegemonic ways."[41] To name the empire is already to begin to challenge it.

The eschatological vision of the Bible brings an irreverence and questioning-ness to any discussion of economic matters. In a world like today's, where an unfettered market system reigns almost unchallenged, the Bible offers a certain disrespect and a sharp critique to any dominant system that causes exclusion and suffering. People of faith, inspired by the vision of another world coming and moved by their solidarity with one another, can have a capacity to confront the excesses and injustices of globalization. They are well placed to play their part in the great movement for change that Arundhati Roy proposes in the following terms:

---

39. *Together towards Life*, §31.

40. Pope Francis, *Evangelii Gaudium*, §56.

41. "Address by the Conference Moderator", in Jukko and Keum, eds., *Moving in the Spirit*, 57–64, at 59.

> Our strategy should be not only to confront Empire, but to lay siege to it. To deprive it of oxygen. To shame it. To mock it. With our art, our music, our literature, our stubbornness, our joy, our brilliance, our sheer relentlessness – and our ability to tell our own stories . . . Remember this: We be many and they be few. They need us more than we need them.[42]

So long as the lives of more than one billion people are blighted by extreme poverty, people who are guided by the biblical vision will occupy a questioning and protesting position vis-à-vis the prevailing economic system. This allies them with many others who, drawing on various religious and secular traditions, find themselves impelled to join the struggle.

A Question of Worship

This brings us inevitably to the question of worship: To what do we ascribe ultimate worth? The words of Jesus to the woman of Samaria carry powerful relevance today: "God is spirit, and those who worship him must worship in spirit and truth" (John 4:24). When the material displaces the spiritual in terms of holding ultimate value, all of life is commodified, the earth is debased, and human life is devalued. This is most obviously apparent to those who find themselves excluded by the concentration of power and resources under the imperial system.

One of the preparatory documents for the Arusha conference considered what this means for evangelism:

> Evangelism today is alert to the asymmetries and imbalances of power that divide and trouble us in church and world. Initiative lies with those who have been excluded by the systemic injustices of the prevailing global system. Those who are cast out to the margins can become agents of transforming evangelism. Those who the gospel is recreating as first fruits of the new heaven and earth are then witnesses against the elitist heaven and despoiled earth embodied by worldly empires. In this respect, evangelism turns the status quo upside down. It subverts the political and religious powers that deny the dignity, diversity and preciousness of all God's creation. It invites all these relationships and systems into a new orientation towards fullness of life. As we live out our discipleship of Christ, we are together for transformation.[43]

---

42. Arundhati Roy, *The Ordinary Person's Guide to Empire* (London: Harper Perennial, 2004), 77.

43. CWME Study Document "Being Disciples Means Sharing Good News," in Risto Jukko, ed., *Conference on World Mission and Evangelism, 2018. Complete Digital Edition of the Arusha*

The longstanding commitment of the ecumenical movement is to witness to an entirely different approach to the distribution of resources. The perspective of Christian faith is that the followers of Jesus are "all receivers in the first instance, and that Christ is the one who gives everything to all."[44] As Dongsung Kim remarks, "This affirmation repudiates an economic model of ownership that is privatized, belittles the sovereignty of God and denies life in community that benefits the common good."[45] Sharing, as a "responsive relation to others, is indeed the costly discipleship to which God calls us and for which Jesus has set the pattern before us."[46] This direction was charted by the 6th WCC Assembly held at Vancouver in 1983 when it stated that "the ministry of sharing" is a challenge to the churches to practise what they are called to be: sharing communities which seek to do justice, taking the side of all those who are denied their share in the fullness of life that God has promised."[47] The path of discipleship leads not only to a posture of protest but to an adventure of sharing resources and building an inclusive community.

A Choice to Be Made

Jesus stated a perennial truth when he said, "No slave can serve two masters; for a slave will either hate the one and love the other, or be devoted to the one and despise the other. You cannot serve God and wealth" (Luke 16:13). Meeting this stark choice is inescapable if we are to be disciples of Jesus. We choose to serve either the living God who gives freely and abundantly or the mammon that will suck the life out of us. To reject the false god of the market system and to choose to worship the God of justice, love, and grace is to offer the kind of witness that expresses the meaning of mission in our time.

Report, 220–32, at 226, https://www.oikoumene.org/en/resources/publications/DigitalEdition_ArushaReport_ALL.pdf).

44. Tracy Early, *Simply Sharing – A Personal Survey of How Well the Ecumenical Movement Shares its Resources* (Geneva: WCC Publications, 1980), 20.

45. Dongsung Kim, "Partnership and Resource-Sharing," in Ross et al., *Ecumenical Missiology*, 259–70, at 261.

46. Ghana Robinson, ed., *Sharing and Living – A Study on the Ecumenical Sharing of Resources in India* (Madurai, India: Nepolean Press, 1983), 2.

47. David Gill, ed., *Gathered for Life: Official Report VI Assembly World Council of Churches Vancouver, Canada, 24 July–10 August 1983* (Geneva: WCC Publications, 1983), 63.

Questions for Reflection

Why does the "market system" come to be treated like a god?

How might you be tempted to worship the market system?

What does it mean in practice to put God first in the living of our lives?

3. A FAITH TO PROCLAIM

We are called to proclaim the good news of Jesus Christ – the fullness of life, the repentance and forgiveness of sin, and the promise of eternal life – in word and deed, in a violent world where many are sacrificed to the idols of death (Jeremiah 32:35) and where many have not yet heard the gospel.

Compelled to Speak

The news about Jesus Christ is so good you cannot keep it to yourself. When you have heard the news, you must pass it on to others. This sense of having a message to proclaim is built into the calling when we hear Jesus say, "follow me," and take the decision to become his disciple. When Paul was reflecting on this calling, he wrote to his friends at Corinth that "knowing the fear of the Lord, we try to persuade others" (2 Cor. 5:11). There was a sense of compulsion in his experience: "For the love of Christ urges us on, because we are convinced that one has died for all; therefore all have died. And he died for all, so that those who live might live no longer for themselves, but for him who died and was raised for them" (2 Cor. 5:14–15). The new life that has come with Christ is of such a quality that it cannot be hidden in a corner. It calls for proclamation; it calls for evangelism.

Such confidence has been challenged and shaken in recent times. There is a perception that evangelism is necessarily aggressive, disrespectful toward others, and liable to sow seeds of conflict. The long-running alliance between the Christian missionary movement and European colonial rule has stoked suspicion in many parts of the world. Some have responded by adopting a relativistic outlook, where everyone is free to follow their own light but must not seek to impose their views on others. Sensitivity to such currents has led to a tendency to downplay the proclamation that looms large in the New Testament.

One of the distinctive features of the WCC's 2013 mission affirmation, *Together towards Life*, is a recovery of confidence in the calling to proclaim the good news of Jesus Christ. It states, "Evangelism is mission activity which makes explicit and unambiguous the centrality of the incarnation, suffering, and resurrection of Jesus Christ without setting limits to the saving grace of God. It seeks to share this good news with all who have not yet heard it and invites them to an experience of life in Christ." This includes "the invitation to personal conversion to a new life in Christ and to discipleship."[48]

In a world that is not always hospitable to this proclamation and invitation, this strikes a note of confidence but not of defensiveness. In fact, Together towards Life includes acknowledgement that the practice of evangelism has sometimes deserved the criticisms that have been levelled at it: "We acknowledge that evangelism at times has been distorted and lost its credibility because some Christians have forced 'conversions' by violent means or the abuse of power."[49] The confident note that rings out from the Arusha Call when it comes to the proclamation of the good news is not to be confused with arrogance or coercion. Humility and a willingness to learn from past mistakes can lay the foundations for responsible, sensitive, and caring evangelism. This is reflected in the important 2011 document, "Christian Witness in a Multi-Religious World: Recommendations for Conduct," jointly issued by the WCC, the Pontifical Council for Interreligious Dialogue and the World Evangelical Alliance.[50]

Together towards Life offered the language of "life" as key to mission and proclamation today, and this is reflected in the language adopted by the Arusha Call. When it summarizes what is to be proclaimed, the first phrase to be offered is "fullness of life," also found in the opening lines of *Together towards Life* and echoing John 10:10. At a time when life itself is at stake, this is invitational language that seeks to be open to all. The Call also acknowledges the reality of sin and our need to receive God's forgiveness in Christ and to embark on a new way of life, before completing its summary with the open horizon of eternal life.

This summary prompts us to recall that Jesus himself was a preacher with a message to declare: "Now after John was arrested, Jesus came to Galilee, proclaiming the good news of God, and saying, "The time is fulfilled, and the kingdom of God has come near; repent, and believe in the good news" (Mark 1:14–15). Those who hear the call to be his disciples have the same message and the same obligation to make it known.

---

48. *Together towards Life*, §80, §81.

49. Ibid., §82.

50. See Chapter 8 below.

Needing to Hear

The good news is not proclaimed into a vacuum. It is addressed in a particular context. Our contemporary context has many features we could consider, but the Arusha Call draws our attention to two in particular. The first is that we find ourselves in "a violent world where many are sacrificed to the idols of death." The second is that it is a world "where many have not yet heard the gospel."

Strong language is used to highlight the violence to which many are subject today. Those who enjoy safety and security struggle to comprehend the reality of those who daily experience violence or the threat of violence. The early 21st century has been a time of war in many contexts, often with civilians, and not just military targets, in the firing line. Technological advances, instead of being used to secure peace, have unleashed yet more devastating forms of violence. Rape has been widely used as a weapon of war. Children have been abducted and forced to become child soldiers. Even in contexts where there is no open warfare, children are vulnerable to human trafficking, forced against their will to become sex slaves.

In view of these realities, we can easily understand why the Arusha Call refers to some chilling words from the prophecy of Jeremiah: "They built the high places of Baal in the valley of the son of Hinnom, to offer up their sons and daughters to Molech, though I did not command them, nor did it enter my mind that they should do this abomination, causing Judah to sin" (Jer. 32:35). Human sacrifice might be thought of as a barbaric practice of ancient times from which we have long departed. Yet such is the commodification of human life in our time that for large numbers of young people their experience is one of being sacrificed, their lives forfeited to the sex trade or other forms of modern slavery.

It is in this context that the calling comes to proclaim good news – news of life instead of death, indeed news of fullness of life. This, however, raises a further challenging reality: many have not had an opportunity to hear the good news. In fact, the uneven distribution of Christians worldwide ensures that many have no opportunity to hear the good news of Jesus Christ through personal contact. The 2009 *Atlas of Global Christianity* found that "Buddhists, Hindus and Muslims have relatively little contact with Christians. In each case, over 86% of these religionists globally do not personally know a Christian."[51] With a missionary mandate that calls them to take the good

---

51. Todd M. Johnson and Kenneth R. Ross, eds, *Atlas of Global Christianity* (Edinburgh: Edinburgh University Press, 2009), 316.

news of Jesus to "the ends of the earth" (Acts 1:8), disciples cannot be complacent about such a situation.

This is a point that has been close to the heart of evangelicals, such as those who belong to the Lausanne Movement. After a period when there appeared to be a polarization between the ecumenical movement with its strong social and political agenda and the evangelical movement with its strong emphasis on personal faith and salvation, today we see a strengthening consensus that both emphases are needed in order to faithfully proclaim the good news of Christ. Hence, we find the WCC's *Together towards Life* mission affirmation quoting from the *Cape Town Commitment* of the Lausanne Movement: "Evangelism is the outflow of hearts that are filled with the love of God for those who do not yet know him."[52]

At the Arusha conference, Jin S. Kim, the pastor of All Nations Church in Minneapolis, USA, took account of our contemporary context and sketched the evangelistic task in these terms:

> Christians are to be called out of a sick society built on the evils of racism, sexism, militarism, exploitation, ecocide and destructive competition. We are to create a new community of love . . . We will have to participate in the broader economic system, but we will not allow capitalist dogma to influence our internal economics. We will draw people from our immediate context of great brokenness, but our mission will include the casting out of imperial demons and the healing of bodies and souls so that we can relate rightly to our God, our neighbours (human and non-human), and God's good green earth.[53]

A Calling for All

An important feature of the Arusha Call is that it is addressed to all who have been baptized and profess to belong to Jesus Christ. The proclamation of the good news is not the exclusive domain of any particular group, such as the clergy. Indeed, the Arusha conference went so far as to say, "Christ's call to discipleship has been distorted when responsibility for Christian witness has been delegated to professionals; baptism is a call to discipleship and we are all called to follow the way of Christ in every dimension of our lives."[54]

The call to be a disciple is inseparable from a calling to evangelize – to spread the good news. The conference found that "across the world church we

52. *Together towards Life*, §81.

53. "The Arusha Conference Report," 9.

54. Ibid., 13.

are living through a rediscovery of the reality that the mandate for evangelism is not restricted to any select group, but is given to all disciples of Jesus Christ. Evangelism is from everyone to everyone, extending to all the invitation to personal conversion to a new life in Christ."[55]

This recognition that the calling to proclaim the good news extends to all disciples was a common theme in three recent major mission statements. In 2010, the Lausanne Movement's *Cape Town Commitment* stated,

> We encourage all believers to accept and affirm their own daily ministry and mission as being wherever God has called them to work . . . We need intensive efforts to train all God's people in whole-life discipleship, which means to live, think, work, and speak from a biblical worldview and with missional effectiveness in every place or circumstance of daily life and work.[56]

In 2012, the WCC's *Together towards Life* affirmed,

> As the church discovers more deeply its identity as a missionary community, its outward-looking character finds expression in evangelism . . . All Christians, churches, and congregations are called to be vibrant messengers of the gospel of Jesus Christ, which is the good news of salvation. Evangelism is a confident but humble sharing of our faith and conviction with other people. Such sharing is a gift to others which announces the love, grace, and mercy of God in Christ.[57]

In 2013, in *Evangelii Gaudium*, Pope Francis expressed the conviction that "all the baptized, whatever their position in the Church or their level of instruction in the faith, are agents of evangelization, and it would be insufficient to envisage a plan of evangelization to be carried out by professionals while the rest of the faithful would simply be passive recipients."[58]

A rediscovery of the reality that the call to discipleship is at the same time a call to evangelism is one of the key drivers of a recovery of missionary impetus for the church in today's world. As the Arusha conference found, "If we wish evangelism to be convincing today, the first thing we must do is to be disciples. Humility and sacrifice are urgently needed to liberate the gospel from

---

55. Ibid., 13.

56. Cape Town Commitment, §II A 3.

57. *Together towards Life*, §79, §8.

58. Pope Francis, *Evangelii Gaudium*, §120.

captivity to projects of self-aggrandizement. The more we are true disciples of Christ, the more effective our evangelism will be."[59]

Integrity of Faith and Life

Such authenticity is required because we live in times when religion has had bad press – often deservedly so. People have been dismayed to see religion used ideologically to undergird political injustice or military aggression. They have noted that adherence to differing faiths often seems to be at the root of the most intractable and destructive conflicts in the modern world. They have also witnessed faith being reduced to a commodity. It is losing its transcendent reference as it is treated as a marketable product to serve the interests of those who "own" it. The abusive and exploitative use of religion has, understandably, caused extensive disillusionment – to the extent that it has become difficult in some quarters even to get a hearing for the good news of Christ.

What is required is not so much a new form of words or a different communication technique as a translation of the gospel into a lived reality that vouches for its authenticity. As mission leader Ken Gnanakan has written,

> While there is need to renew our allegiance to proclaim the word faithfully, there is greater need to flesh the message out in acts that express this kingdom. Proclamation is urgent, but demonstration is the priority. The world must hear the message of the Kingdom, but it will also want to see some concrete demonstration of this message.[60]

Hence the Arusha Call makes the point that the good news must be proclaimed not in word only but also in deed.

Here is where the integral relation between evangelism and discipleship makes all the difference. The message to be proclaimed and the life to be lived need to be consistent with one another. The integrity of the faith depends on a corresponding way of life. Evangelism, in this perspective, is a matter of being before it is a matter of doing.

The preparatory paper on evangelism prepared for the Arusha conference reflected on this in light of what we learn from the gospels of the approach taken by Jesus himself:

---

59. "The Arusha Conference Report," 13.

60. Ken Gnanakan, "To Proclaim the Good News of the Kingdom," in *Mission in the 21st Century: Exploring the Five Marks of Global Mission*, ed. Andrew Walls and Cathy Ross (London: Darton, Longman and Todd, 2008), 9.

Jesus made a practice of spending time with his disciples. This was the essence of his training programme – letting his disciples follow him. Knowledge of Christ was gained by association before it was understood by explanation. He ate with his disciples, slept near them, and talked with them. ... Jesus gave himself away to his disciples by imparting to them everything that God had given to him.[61]

In the perspective of the Arusha conference, "When evangelism seeks conversion, it means change in the evangelist as well as the evangelized. It is not to be understood as manipulating someone else into my own likeness. Rather, together we are called toward new life in Christ, calling the whole creation to abundant life in inclusive community."[62] The approach taken by Jesus sets the tone for his disciples. When evangelism is done in Christ's way, writes Claudia Währisch-Oblau, "it will be humble, relational, dialogical and respectful of other religions and different cultural practices."[63] Far from evangelism being a matter of imposing one's beliefs on a reluctant recipient, it is a matter of mutual transformation as we learn from one another more about the meaning of the coming of Christ. What is indispensable in doing mission is respect for the other human being, because with respect, a human being can keep his or her dignity in any situation. On this understanding of the task of mission, the love that makes for community is at the same time the action of evangelism.

Questions for Reflection

What do you think is *good* and *news* in the good news of Jesus Christ?

What is involved in proclaiming the good news in both *word and deed*?

What forms of violence are affecting people in today's world?

---

61. "Being Disciples Means Sharing Good News," 221–22. See also Knud Jørgensen, *Equipping for Service: Christian Leadership in Church and Society* (Oxford: Regnum, 2012), 29.

62. "The Arusha Conference Report," 13.

63. Claudia Währisch-Oblau, "Evangelism," in Ross et al., *Ecumenical Missiology*, 151–66, at 165.

4. WORKING FROM THE MARGINS

We are called to joyfully engage in the ways
of the Holy Spirit, who empowers people
from the margins with agency, in the search
for justice and dignity (Acts 1:8; 4:31).

The Spirit of Joy

The Conference on World Mission and Evangelism in Arusha took *"Moving in the Spirit"* as the first part of its title, striking the spiritual note that has been a hallmark of mission thinking in the 21st century. "Come, Holy Spirit, heal and reconcile" was the theme of the 2005 WCC Conference on World Mission and Evangelism in Athens, the immediate predecessor of Arusha.[64] It was noted at the time that this was the first Conference on World Mission and Evangelism to be hosted in a predominantly Orthodox country, thus exposing it to the strong theology of the Holy Spirit that has been a distinctive feature of the Orthodox tradition. At the same time, the Athens conference was marked by a broadening of participation, particularly to include greater representation of evangelicals and Pentecostals. The latter have put openness to the Holy Spirit at the heart of church life, something that has struck a chord in many places and made Pentecostalism the fastest growing form of church life in our time.[65] Its emphasis on the Holy Spirit has been increasingly influential in the wider ecumenical movement.

In much of the global South, people are alert to the realm of the spirit, and renewal movements have often been marked by attempts to recover the spiritual dynamism of the New Testament in preference to the more cerebral direction that Christianity seemed to take in Europe. Meanwhile, in the global North it appears that many have grown tired of dogmatic expressions of Christian faith yet remain open to the spiritual dimension of life.[66] Globally, it seemed that the time was ripe for a recovery of the sense of the life and action of the Holy Spirit that distinguished the Christian faith from its beginnings.

---

64. Jacques Matthey, ed., *Come Holy Spirit, Heal and Reconcile! Called in Christ to Be Reconciling and Healing Communities – Report of the WCC Conference on World Mission and Evangelism, Athens, Greece, May 9–16, 2005* (Geneva: WCC Publications, 2008).

65. See, for example, Allan Anderson, *An Introduction to Pentecostalism* (Cambridge: Cambridge University Press, 2004).

66. See further Gerrit Noort, Kyriaki Avtzi, and Stefan Paas, eds, *Sharing Good News: Handbook on Evangelism in Europe* (Geneva: WCC Publications, 2017).

Such a recovery is evident in the 2013 WCC mission affirmation, *Together towards Life*, which, like never before, places the Holy Spirit at the front and centre of our understanding of mission. Amongst its opening affirmations is the following:

> Life in the Holy Spirit is the essence of mission, the core of why we do what we do and how we live our lives. Spirituality gives the deepest meaning to our lives and motivates our actions. It is a sacred gift from the Creator, the energy for affirming and caring for life. This mission spirituality has a dynamic of transformation which, through the spiritual commitment of people, is capable of transforming the world in God's grace.[67]

Expressing mission in terms of the living of life and striking a spiritual note paved the way for the renewed attention to discipleship that came with the Arusha Conference.

As the Arusha Call summons us to engage in the ways of the Holy Spirit, it adds the qualification that this is something to be done joyfully. Amongst the fruit of the Spirit is joy (Gal. 5:22). While it can be costly and painful at times to be a disciple, still it remains always a calling marked by joy. This was something memorably captured by Pope Francis in his 2013 encyclical *Evangelii Gaudium*, which begins with the words, "The joy of the gospel fills the hearts and lives of all who encounter Jesus. Those who accept his offer of salvation are set free from sin, sorrow, inner emptiness and loneliness. With Christ joy is constantly born anew." He further observes, "our technological society has succeeded in multiplying occasions of pleasure, yet has found it very difficult to engender joy."[68] With the joy that comes from life in the Holy Spirit, disciples can bring to the world something for which it is longing.

From the Margins

Historically, mission has often been imagined as a movement initiated from a strong centre and reaching out to places on the periphery. Recent mission thinking has radically reversed this perspective, suggesting that the mission of God begins from the margins and frequently brings a challenge to those at the centre. As *Together towards Life* states,

---

67. *Together towards Life*, §3.

68. Pope Francis, *Evangelii Gaudium*, §1.

Mission has been understood as a movement taking place from the centre to the periphery, and from the privileged to the marginalized of society. Now people at the margins are claiming their key role as agents of mission and affirming mission as transformation. This reversal of roles in the envisioning of mission has strong biblical foundations because God chose the poor, the foolish, and the powerless (1 Cor. 1:18–31) to further God's mission of justice and peace so that life may flourish.[69]

It was very clear that the notion of "mission from the margins" captured the imagination of the Arusha conference. However, it also proved to be a somewhat slippery concept, not easy to define; and therefore it sometimes brought an edge of frustration to the discussion. The Arusha conference nonetheless adopted this line of thinking as a critical missional perspective for our time:

In an unjust and exclusionary world, the gospel of Christ continues to rise from the margins and challenge the mighty to lay down their power and make way for the coming of justice. The gospel of Christ breaks out from communities that are despised but that turn out to be the most important of all. To that extent, mission from the margins is not a mere option, but an essential way of collaborating with God in today's world.[70]

Deenabandhu Manchala has attempted to give meaning to the concept of the margins by explaining it in terms of examples of people and contexts where it is a reality:

A necessary first step, therefore, is to come to an awareness of the faces and names of those who we refer to as the margins. A cursory look at some of these would reveal the truth about the reasons for their marginalization. The hundreds and thousands of refugees of war from Africa, the Middle East, and many parts of the world, the Palestinians who are punished for their resistance to occupation, the African Americans who are pushed further to make space for white privilege, the aboriginal Australians and the First Nation people in the Americas whose faces are veiled to hide the historical crimes, the children who are trafficked and are fleeing in order to escape the wars of the drug lords in Central America, women who are deprived of education and employment, and even the right to life, in many parts of the world, the Pacific Islanders who live on the brink of being submerged, the nearly 90,000 war widows in Sri Lanka, millions of rural and urban poor, forced migrant workers, child labourers, climate refugees, physically disabled people and people maimed

---

69. *Together towards Life,* §6.

70. "The Arusha Conference Report," 12.

in wars and land mines, and the nearly 250 million discriminated Dalits in South Asia.[71]

The Arusha conference was sensitive to such realities:

> Indigenous peoples continue to suffer discrimination and exploitation at the hands of the powerful, yet their wisdom may hold the key to the future. Despite advances in gender awareness worldwide, women continue to be treated unequally and to suffer painfully at the hands of male power. Minority groups in many contexts experience discrimination, their culture and their very humanity treated with scant respect.[72]

The conference was aware that inequality and injustice have often been highlighted, yet it was energized by a sense of initiative – now is the time to act and transformation can come through mission from the margins.

The Agency of Mission

This discussion has put a focus on the agency of mission: Who are the agents that make mission happen? This question is being answered in a radical way, subverting the assumption that the powerful and the well-resourced are best placed to be the agents of mission. An alternative vision gripped the attention of the Arusha conference when it heard from Adi Mariana Waqa, a young woman from the Pacific, who was the main speaker at a plenary session on mission from the margins. She declared,

> I am Adi Mariana Waqa, I am poor, I am bound, I am unfavoured, I am oppressed! But I am a precious child made in the image of God. I have agency, I am worthy, I have a voice, and I am free! I am free because I live and walk in the Spirit! I am free and I joyfully bear God's good news and hope as Christ's disciple from the margins transforming the world. Thanks be to God!"[73]

Mission from the margins means people like Adi Mariana Waqa draw confidence from their faith and discipleship to become agents of transformation in the world.

---

71. Deenabandhu Manchala, "Margins," in Ross et al., *Ecumenical Missiology*, 309–19, at 312.

72. "The Arusha Conference Report," 12.

73. Ibid., 12.

The question of agency has a long history in the study of Christian mission. One of the sharpest critiques of the Western missionary movement was published by Anglican missionary Roland Allen more than 100 years ago. In a book called *Missionary Methods: St Paul's or Ours?* Allen contrasted the Pauline mission, which was powerless in worldly terms and therefore dependent on the Holy Spirit, with what he saw as the alliance of the modern missionary movement with the power of the Western world.[74] Were Allen alive today, he might be surprized to see that the identification of Christianity with the powerful is increasingly a thing of the past. More and more, the agents of Christian mission come from among the weak, the broken, and the vulnerable. It is a new kind of agency; but is it not one that has greater affinity to Paul – and to Jesus – than the form of missionary presence that often appeared to be allied with imperial power and economic exploitation? Increasingly, we see a situation emerging that is quite opposite to the one that troubled Roland Allen.

Swept by unmerciful currents of history, Christian believers bear witness to the suffering Lord in whom they find the strength to meet adversity. A new (or recovered) pattern of missionary activity is emerging in which the poor take the gospel to the rich. Africa is the world's poorest continent and, unsurprisingly, the one from which the greatest number of migrants originate. It is also the continent with the most vibrant expansion of Christian faith. Hence, many migrants come from the new heartlands of Christianity and bring the flame of faith to the old centres in the North, where the fire is burning low. As Tokunboh Adeyemo of Kenya, General Secretary of the Association of Evangelicals in Africa, has remarked, Africa has made the transition "from mission field to missionary force."[75]

It is hard to say what the effect of this 21st century movement of mission will be, but it certainly already looks very different from the one that prevailed in the 19th and 20th centuries. The organizational pattern of mission also starts to look quite different from that which prevailed in the Western missionary movement. There is no head office, no organizing committee, no command structure, no centralized fund, no comprehensive strategic direction. It appears to be a disorganized movement of individuals making their own connections, developing their own perspectives, and functioning within networks they themselves have constructed. How could the older missionary movement productively relate to the new pattern? What forms of connection

---

74. Roland Allen, *Missionary Methods: St Paul's or Ours? A Study of the Church in the Four Provinces* (London: Robert Scott, 1912).

75. Tokunboh Adeyemo, cited in Jehu J. Hanciles, *Beyond Christendom: Globalization, African Migration and the Transformation of the West* (Maryknoll: Orbis, 2008), 218.

and association will provide unity and synergy for such a diverse movement of faith?

Mission from the margins means a rethink on all sides, both from the powerful and the powerless. As Stephen Bevans reflects on the Arusha conference, he suggests,

> Discipleship today for those accustomed to privilege and power needs to be about letting go, recognizing that the real power for God's mission is at the margins of society and the margins of the church. In the same way, discipleship today for those on the margins is having the courage to claim the power and articulate the wisdom that is there.[76]

Justice and Dignity

The Arusha Call indicates what gives direction to mission from the margins – the search for justice and dignity. This surely strikes a chord with the many who are on the receiving end of injustice and who find that their human dignity is under threat. It also sets a course of confrontation with vested interests. Deenabandhu Manchala explains that the mission from the margins "involves confronting cultures and systems, and transforming them through just and life-affirming alternatives. Unfortunately, these forces and cultures are also present and even rampant in many churches. An option such as this necessitates introspection and transformation within."[77] Churches themselves have to be prepared to face this challenge and be themselves transformed before they can become agents of God's transformation in the world.

Meanwhile, those on the margins need not wait for anyone from the "centre" to come to their aid. *Together towards Life* affirms,

> People on the margins have agency, and can often see what, from the centre, is out of view. People on the margins, living in vulnerable positions, often know what exclusionary forces are threatening their survival and can best discern the urgency of their struggles; people in positions of privilege have much to learn from the daily struggles of people living in marginal conditions.[78]

Very often marginalized people are meeting complex and challenging circumstances; but to be a disciple is to live a life of unquenchable hope. As *Together towards Life* puts it, "Through struggles in and for life, marginalized

---

76. Bevans, "Transforming Discipleship," 367.

77. Manchala, "Margins," 314.

78. *Together towards Life,* §38.

people are reservoirs of the active hope, collective resistance, and perseverance that are needed to remain faithful to the promised reign of God."[79] This is the direction that leads to justice and dignity. As Jesus promised in the Sermon on the Mount, "Blessed are those who hunger and thirst for righteousness, for they will be filled" (Matthew 5:6).

Questions for Reflection

What does life look like when it has joy?

Who are the marginalized people in the place where you live?

What does it mean to have "agency"?

---

79. *Together towards Life,* §39.

5. DISCERNING THE WORD OF GOD

We are called to discern the word of God in a world that communicates many contradictory, false, and confusing messages.

Time for Discernment

When Jesus' call to discipleship first went out, his followers soon became aware that they would need to exercise discernment in their spiritual life. As John urged his readers, "Beloved, do not believe every spirit, but test the spirits to see whether they are from God; for many false prophets have gone out into the world" (1 John 4:1). *Together towards Life* stresses the importance of such discernment in our time: "We discern the Spirit of God wherever life in its fullness is affirmed and in all its dimensions, including liberation of the oppressed, healing and reconciliation of broken communities, and the restoration of creation. We also discern evil spirits wherever forces of death and destruction of life prevail."[80] This opens up a challenging journey. *Together towards Life* continues:

> The churches are called to discern the work of the life-giving Spirit sent into the world and to join with the Holy Spirit in bringing about God's reign of justice (Acts 1:6–8). When we have discerned the Holy Spirit's presence, we are called to respond, recognizing that God's Spirit is often subversive, leading us beyond boundaries and surprising us.[81]

The Arusha Call, in this section, highlights the contested environment in which we hear God's message, amidst siren voices that would contradict and deny it. We can only hear the word from within the world in which we are set. Therefore, we need to be alert to forces that would distort and corrupt our understanding. Without active discernment, we will not be able to discover what God has to say to us.

---

80. *Together towards Life*, §24.

81. *Ibid.*, §25.

The Word and the World

Word and world are juxtaposed at this point in "The Arusha Call to Discipleship." This takes us into the core of the meaning of mission. As Stephen Bevans and Roger Schroeder explain, "Mission . . . is the church's witness to faith in certain *constants* – the person and work of Jesus Christ, ecclesial existence in eschatological hope of a salvation that embraces the whole of humanity and of human culture – always within particular and ever-changing contexts."[82]

The Arusha Call draws urgency from the fact that the global context today is marked by messages that are likely to distort or detract from the constants of the message entrusted to the church. The advent of the Internet and the rise of social media have created an environment where people are bombarded by messaging all the time. Discernment is required if we are to apprehend the word that comes from God amidst the surrounding cacophony.

The kind of discernment that is needed has been captured in the phrase "prophetic dialogue." At first sight this might sound like a self-contradictory expression. Prophets we imagine as people with great conviction about what they have to say. Dialogue is a more tentative approach, where a listening posture is adopted. Stephen Bevans suggests that both are needed if mission is to take effect.

First, there can be no mission without meaningful human connections. Hence, dialogue is essential. "This basic attitude or spirituality of dialogue is the *sine qua non* of intercultural mission. Only when those engaged in mission are open to the women and men among whom they work, only when they allow themselves to learn from and be challenged by those among they minister, can the full impact of intercultural mission be experienced and profited from."[83] There needs to be a deep listening, a deep sharing of human experience and friendship. The missionary must be learner before they can be teacher. They need to profoundly identify with the context and people, learning to appreciate and growing to love them. This is a journey of exchange, of dialogue, of coming to understand and appreciate one another.

The second dimension of the missionary calling is the prophetic one. There is need to discern points of engagement that can be addressed by the biblical message. Those committed to mission find a way

---

82. Stephen B. Bevans and Roger P. Schroeder, *Constants in Context: A Theology of Mission for Today* (Maryknoll: Orbis, 2004), 349.

83. Stephen Bevans, "Prophetic Dialogue and Intercultural Mission," in *Intercultural Mission*, ed. Lazar T. Stanislaus and Martin Üffing (Sankt Augustin: Steyler Missionswissenschaft Institut; and Delhi: ISPCK, 2015), 201–14, at 205–206.

of communicating the gospel message that is clear and focused, relevant and powerful, one that engages people's lives and the cultures in which they live. They speak out as well in all sorts of ways against evil in society – individuals in daily encounters, in editorials, in blogs and tweets; communities in statements of opposition of oppressive laws or cultural elements; the institutional church in statements that condemn political injustice, ecological destruction, economic exploitation, or religious intolerance.[84]

Here, we see an element of challenge, even confrontation, as the light of Christ exposes all kinds of darkness. In every culture, Christ's call is a call to conversion and to a new life. The calling of mission is to live and speak out that call.

When this prophetic calling is combined with sensitivity to the need for dialogue, what emerges can be described as prophetic dialogue. This, as Bevans and Cathy Ross observe, "is no easy task. It requires discipline – spiritual discipline."[85] On the one hand, it involves the deep listening that enables us to learn from others, and on the other hand, it means clarifying our own understanding in such a way as to enable us to fulfil a prophetic role. In this way, word and world are brought together. In truth, these were never far removed from one another. For there are seeds of the word in human life and history and the Spirit of God is present in the experience of every people. So the world in which we live is one in which God's presence and message are already embedded. Yet, the need remains for that message to be announced and to bring its challenge to every situation. Discerning the word of God is therefore the constant task of those called to discipleship.

Contradiction and Confusion

As the Arusha Call takes account of our global context, one point it highlights is the extent to which in today's situation we hear many contradictory, false, and confusing messages. It is surely not accidental that the Oxford Dictionary's Word of the Year for 2016 was "post-truth."[86] During that year, a common explanation for what was taking place was that we were living in a "post-truth era" – in particular, an era of post-truth politics. At first sight,

---

84. Bevans, "Prophetic Dialogue and Intercultural Mission," 207.

85. Stephen B. Bevans and Cathy Ross, "Introduction: Mission as Prophetic Dialogue," in *Mission on the Road to Emmaus: Constants, Context and Prophetic Dialogue*, ed. Cathy Ross and Stephen B. Bevans (London: SCM, 2015), xvii.

86. OxfordLanguages website (Oxford University Press, 2020), https://en.oxforddictionaries.com/word-of-the-year/word-of-the-year-2016.

this is a curious word to add to our language. Truth, surely, is always going to exist: How could we be in an era where truth has been left behind? Of course, there will always be objective criteria available to distinguish true from false. But the point about "post-truth" is that it describes a state of affairs where whether or not something is objectively true no longer matters. The veracity of a statement is unimportant or irrelevant. If it appeals to emotion and affirms a given perception, then the statement has had its intended effect.

There can be little doubt that the reason the term "post-truth" has gained currency in recent times lies in the nature of the pro-leave tactics in the UK's referendum on membership in the European Union and of Donald Trump's presidential campaign in the United States. In earlier times, if a politician were found to have stated something that was demonstrably false, their credibility would collapse and their cause would be lost. In a post-truth situation, a politician can carry on repeating a claim even after convincing independent analysis has shown it to be untrue. As journalist John Lanchester observed following the referendum on EU membership, "I don't think there has ever been a time in British politics when so many people in public life spent so much time loudly declaring things they knew not to be true."[87] The point, however, is that whereas once it would have been fatal to one's political prospects to be found to be deliberately lying, in a post-truth era it is possible for politicians who have achieved their ends through being untruthful to be rewarded and to flourish.

No wonder that another word that has been trending is "Orwellian," referring to George Orwell and particularly his novel *Nineteen Eighty-Four*, which traces the emergence of an authoritarian "big brother" of society.[88] Orwell's point was that a key element in constructing an authoritarian society is to manipulate language and use propaganda so that what is false comes to be accepted as true and society's entire perception is reconstructed to serve the interests of those in power.

The loss of high standards of truthfulness in political life thus becomes a tool in the hands of authoritarian, populist leaders. Truth and power, however, are not only political issues but also religious ones. As regards truth, the Christian vision offers a perception of reality that arises from obedience to Christ. In the post-Enlightenment Western world, the challenge to Christian discipleship has been how to express that vision of faith in a context where

---

87. John Lanchester, "Brexit Blues," *London Review of Books* 38:15 (28 July 2016), 3–6, at 6.

88. George Orwell, *Nineteen Eighty-Four* (London: Secker and Warburg, 1949).

great authority was accorded to human reason. That authority is now being diminished as we enter a post-truth era. The Christian vision now has to be advanced in a context where the raw assertion of power by authoritarian regimes creates a climate that in many ways is antithetical to biblical faith. Power as domination and control stands in contrast to power as love and service. As the "Edinburgh 2010 Common Call" stated, "Disturbed by the asymmetries and imbalances of power that divide and trouble us in church and world, we are called to repentance, to critical reflection on systems of power, and to accountable use of power structures."[89] The hermeneutic of suspicion with regard to the exercise of power that is built into the Christian tradition may be crucial to faithful witness in our time. In particular, to heed the biblical teaching to "let your 'yes' be yes and your 'no' be no" (James 5:12) will mean taking the path of costly discipleship.

Bold Humility

The Arusha Call's reference to discernment carries the implication that it will not always be easy to form a judgment on what the gospel of Christ means and demands in a given situation. We need to struggle over weighing up different options and determining what is the true path of discipleship. Lesslie Newbigin once reflected,

> It was one of the very great gifts of Reinhold Niebuhr that he could illuminate both the disastrous consequences of introducing a Christian absolute into politics, and at the same time the absolute obligation of Christians to discern the relative less or more of justice and freedom, and to commit themselves to action on behalf of that which was relatively better.[90]

Such discernment involves navigating ambiguity and evaluating alternatives in order to discover, test, and embrace what is required by the call to follow Jesus.

One key resource is that the exercise of discernment is not one that we have to undertake alone. For the call to discipleship is one that calls us into community, and it is as a community struggling together that we find our

---

89. "Edinburgh 2010 Common Call," §4, in Kirsteen Kim and Andrew Anderson, eds, *Edinburgh 2010: Mission Today and Tomorrow* (Oxford: Regnum, 2011), 1; cited in *Together towards Life,* §33.

90. Lesslie Newbigin, *The Other Side of 1984: Questions for the Churches* (Geneva: WCC, 1983), 42.

way forward. As Olav Fykse Tveit, the then general secretary of the WCC, asked at the Arusha conference, "How to find the way the Spirit moves? The ecumenical experience has taught us: by listening to the word of God together and learning from one another. There is no way to say that I alone or we alone know the way the wind is blowing. Nobody knows where the wind is blowing, Jesus says (John 3)."[91] We need humility and reverence, acknowledging the mystery of the working of the Spirit and our profound dependence on one another. Tveit concludes, "It is only in sharing what the Spirit is doing and has done in our churches and communities and in our encounters with others that makes us able to discern this together."[92]

This discerning of the word of God is closely bound up with living an authentic life of discipleship. Lesslie Newbigin once made this clear by painting a vivid picture of his own attempts to discern and proclaim God's word during his service in south India:

> I have often stood at the door of a little church, with the Christian congregation seated on the ground in the middle of a great circle of Hindus and Muslims standing around. As I have opened the Scriptures and tried to preach the Word of God to them, I have always known that my words would carry little weight, would only be believed, if those standing around could recognize in those seated in the middle that the promises of God were being fulfilled; if they could see that this new community in the village represented a new kind of body in which the old divisions of caste and education and temperament were being transcended in a new form of brotherhood. If they could not see anything of the kind, they would not be likely to believe.[93]

Discerning and declaring the word of God is not something we can credibly do without the witness of a corresponding way of life. There is an intellectual struggle to discover what God is saying in a given context, but this struggle is inseparably interwoven with the ethical commitment of a faithful life of discipleship.

In a world where many different claims are loudly asserted, we might hesitate to advance the claims of Christ or even to be sure ourselves that we know what the word of God is saying in a particular context. It is appropriate to

---

91. Olav Fykse Tveit, "Opening Address," in Jukko and Keum, eds., *Moving in the Spirit*, 50–56, at 55.

92. Ibid., 55.

93. Lesslie Newbigin, *Is Christ Divided? A Plea for Christian Unity in a Revolutionary Age*, (Grand Rapids: Eerdmans, 1961), 24; cited in Bevans and Schroeder, *Constants in Context*, 365.

be humble, but this does not mean that we have to be lacking in confidence. David Bosch once captured the balance that makes for convincing witness. He affirmed:

> that we do not have all the answers and are prepared to live within the framework of penultimate knowledge, that we regard our involvement in dialogue and mission as an adventure, are prepared to take risks, and are anticipating surprises as the Spirit guides us into fuller understanding. This is not opting for agnosticism, but for humility. It is, however, a bold humility – or a humble boldness. We know only in part, but we do know. And we believe that the faith we profess is both true and just, and should be proclaimed. We do this, however, not as judges or lawyers, but as witnesses; not as soldiers, but as envoys of peace; not as high-pressure sales-persons, but as ambassadors of the Servant Lord.[94]

The bold humility that Bosch calls for requires a listening, dialogical approach that is respectful and open to learning from dialogue partners. Yet at the same time it must be an approach that is confident in the message it has to convey, in the word it has to preach.

Questions for Reflection

What messages do you hear "the world" communicating today?

How do you decide when to say no to some powerful messaging?

What gives you confidence that you have discovered what God is saying?

---

94. David J. Bosch, *Transforming Mission: Paradigm Shifts in Theology of Mission* (New York: Orbis, 1991), 489.

6. CARING FOR CREATION

We are called to care for God's creation,
and to be in solidarity with nations severely affected
by climate change in the face of a ruthless
human-centered exploitation of the environment
for consumerism and greed.

Creation and Mission

Until recently, concern for the natural order was often absent from the prevailing understanding of Christian mission. The focus was on the salvation offered to humankind through the coming, dying, and rising of Jesus Christ and the new interhuman relationships that this makes possible. Questions concerning the salvation and reconciliation of human beings were abstracted from the earth that gives them life. There was, therefore, little evidence of concern among proponents of Christian mission for the integrity of the natural order. Moreover, this was not only a sin of omission. The Western missionary movement was closely allied with a commercial enterprise that sought to make profit from new resources and new markets, giving little thought to the future of the environment. The ecological crisis now finding expression in rapid global warming has exposed the inadequacy of a vision of the future that overlooked the threats to the planet posed by the expansion of the modern industrial economy.[95]

The extent of the calamity already taking effect through climate change, water scarcity, rising sea levels, and desertification has awoken mission thinkers and strategists to a challenge ignored for too long. It has provoked a rereading of the Bible and a rediscovery of the fundamental reality that God loves the whole creation and embraces it in the divine saving purposes. We have moved from a personal to a cosmic view of salvation that is far-reaching in its implications for mission. It has led to practical repentance as individuals have examined their lifestyles and adopted more responsible and sustainable ways of life. It has generated missionary initiatives that have stewardship of the environment at their heart. Each context is engaged in a way that takes full account of its ecological dimensions. Restoring a sound relationship with

---

95. See further Ernst M. Conradie, *Christianity and Earthkeeping: In Search of an Inspiring Vision* (Stellenbosch: Sun Press, 2011).

the earth forms a key strand in a viable missionary strategy for our time. Caring for creation, as a theological imperative, may be a key way to witness to Christ and commend the gospel in today's world.

This was a concern powerfully adopted by *Together towards Life* when it took up the theme of "Mission and the flourishing of creation." It offered a close theological integration of two spheres of thought that have often been kept apart:

> Mission is the overflow of the infinite love of the Triune God. God's mission begins with the act of creation. Creation's life and God's life are entwined. The mission of God's Spirit encompasses us all in an ever-giving act of grace. We are therefore called to move beyond a narrowly human-centred approach and to embrace forms of mission which express our reconciled relationship with all created life.[96]

The Arusha conference echoed this concern: "To be worthy missionary disciples, we need to be open to the wonder and mystery of creation, transformed by its beauty and called to action by its suffering. God has given us the responsibility to care for the earth: its natural resources and our environment."[97]

Significant leadership in this theological rediscovery has been offered by Orthodox Christians, with Ecumenical Patriarch Bartholomew becoming known as the "Green Patriarch." Orthodox theology has maintained a close integration of creation, humanity, and redemption during a period when Western Christianity became focused on personal and ecclesial matters and allowed nature to be considered on a secular basis. Orthodox theologians have remained attentive to the Pauline and the Johannine texts that envision a redemption that encompasses the whole creation. Hope for humanity is framed in the context of cosmic redemption. Such a theological vision prevents a narrowing of the question of salvation to the human situation and puts the future of the entire created order at the heart of the faith.

In his 2015 encyclical *Laudato Si'*, Pope Francis exposed the shortcomings of the modern Enlightenment view of the natural world and called for a very different vision of reality.[98] He outlines the difference between thinking in terms of "nature" and thinking in terms of "creation": "Nature is usually seen as a system which can be studied, understood and controlled, whereas

---

96. *Together towards Life,* §19.

97. "The Arusha Conference Report," 11.

98. Pope Francis, *Laudato Si': On Care for Our Common Home,* 24 May (Rome: Vatican Press, 2015), §115, http://www.vatican.va/content/francesco/en/encyclicals/documents/papa-francesco_20150524_enciclica-laudato-si.html.

creation can only be understood as a gift from the outstretched hand of the Father of all, and as a reality illuminated by the love which calls us together into universal communion.[99]

> *Together towards Life* also takes up this emphasis:

> Our participation in mission, our being in creation, and our practice of the life of the Spirit need to be woven together, for they are mutually transformative. We ought not to seek the one without the others. If we do, we will lapse into an individualistic spirituality that leads us to believe falsely that we can belong to God without belonging to our neighbour, and we will fall into a spirituality that simply makes us feel good while other parts of creation hurt and yearn.[100]

The challenge is to bring together our understanding of creation and our understanding of mission like never before.

Climate Justice

This direction of travel receives even more impetus when we consider the injustice that lies at the heart of climate change: those who have done least to cause climate change suffer most from its damaging effects. As Philip Alston, United Nations Special Rapporteur on extreme poverty and human rights, reported in June 2019,

> Climate change will have devastating consequences for people in poverty. Even under the best-case scenario, hundreds of millions will face food insecurity, forced migration, disease, and death. Climate change threatens the future of human rights and risks undoing the last fifty years of progress in development, global health, and poverty reduction.[101]

Meanwhile the greatest culprits tend to be the least affected. This raises a profound ecumenical issue. As Ernst Conradie explains,

> While Christians in some contexts contribute disproportionally to carbon emissions, Christians in other contexts are or will increasingly become the victims of

---

99. Ibid., §76.

100. *Together towards Life*, §21.

101. Philip Alston, *Climate Change and Poverty: Report of the Special Rapporteur on Extreme Poverty and Human Rights* (New York: United Nations, Human Rights Council, 2019), 1.

climate change. Given the way in which political power blocks tend to protect their own interests in negotiations on climate change, it is sad to note that ecumenical fellowship between churches and Christians living in such countries are unable to bridge such divides through common witness, a quest for justice and peace-making . . . Clearly, the quality of fellowship between churches provides a test case for the credibility of their witness to the mission of the Triune God in the world.[102]

Justice for the poor and care for creation are two concerns that go hand in hand. A voice from the Pacific put this challenge to the Arusha conference when Upolu Vaai from Fiji addressed the opening plenary:

> I would go further to call on the church not to limit its theology of mission to the idea of evangelizing people for the sake of nurturing disciples, but to make sure that its mission is able to locate and openly critique the "economy of the one" that is at the heart of poverty and ecological destruction as well as... to produce an eco-relational theology of mission that is Spirit-driven. One that is able to link the suffering of the vulnerable to poverty and ecological annihilation, and that is transformative and subversive to promote the "economy of life."[103]

A significant gesture was made by the youthful participants in the Global Ecumenical Theological Institute (GETI), who brought an important contribution to the Arusha conference. During their pre-conference programme, they planted 12 Mringaringa trees on the campus of the nearby Tumaini University, Makumira. Another meaningful gesture was the re-usable water bottles that were issued to conference participants, without which thousands of empty plastic bottles would have been left in Tanzania. These may be small gestures, but they manifest a new consciousness, a change of heart.

Regarding Christians who are indifferent to this crisis, Pope Francis suggests, "What they all need is an 'ecological conversion' whereby the effects of their encounter with Jesus Christ becomes evident in their relationship to the world around them. Living our vocation to be protectors of God's handiwork is essential to a life of virtue; it is not an optional or secondary aspect of our Christian experience."[104] *As Together towards Life* states, "Humanity cannot be saved alone while the rest of the created world perishes. Eco-justice cannot be

---

102. Ernst Conradie, "Environment," in Ross et al., *Ecumenical Missiology*, 320–30, at 330.

103. Upolu Vaai, "A Call for an Eco-relational Theology of Mission" (response during the Opening Plenary), in Risto Jukko, ed., *Conference on World Mission and Evangelism, 2018. Complete Digital Edition of the Arusha Report*, 77–79, at 79, https://www.oikoumene.org/en/resources/publications/DigitalEdition_ArushaReport_ALL.pdf.

104. Pope Francis, *Laudato Si'*, §217.

separated from salvation, and salvation cannot come without a new humility that respects the needs of all life on earth."[105]

Consumerism and Greed

The Arusha Call does not mince words when it comes to explaining the exploitation of the earth that has led to climate change. It is down to human factors: consumerism and greed. As *Together towards Life* puts the question,

> We want to affirm our spiritual connection with creation, yet the reality is that the earth is being polluted and exploited. Consumerism triggers not limitless growth but rather endless exploitation of the earth's resources. Human greed is contributing to global warming and other forms of climate change. If this trend continues and earth is fatally damaged, what can we imagine salvation to be?[106]

Dismayed by the failure of adults to adopt an appropriate level of urgency in relation to climate change, children took the initiative in 2019 by going "on strike" from school on Fridays to raise awareness that their future is at stake when it comes to tackling the causes of climate change. Writing in *The Guardian*, Greta Thunberg and 46 youth activists set out their case:

> We don't feel like we have a choice: it's been years of talking, countless negotiations, empty deals on climate change and fossil fuel companies being given free rides to drill beneath our soils and burn away our futures for their profit. Politicians have known about climate change for decades. They have willingly handed over their responsibility for our future to profiteers whose search for quick cash threatens our very existence. We have learned that if we don't start acting for our future, nobody else will make the first move. We are the ones we've been waiting for.[107]

The action taken by the children resonates strongly with the Arusha Call. Many good reasons exist for acting to combat climate change. Not the least of them is the call to transforming discipleship.

---

105. *Together towards Life,* §23.

106. Ibid.

107. Greta Thunberg and 46 youth activists, "Young People Have Led the Climate Strikes. Now We Need Adults to Join Us Too," *The Guardian*, 23 May 2019.

Called to Care

Children are taking a much-needed lead. But the Arusha conference also pointed to another source of wisdom: "We have much to learn from Indigenous people, who have demonstrated a greater level of respect for our Mother Earth, recognizing that pollution from the use of fossil fuels and other mineral extractions does not bring honour and is not beneficial to nature and the long-term survival of the inhabitants of the earth."[108] Here, there is much humble pie to be eaten. The industrialized nations, which long assumed they were the champions of progress and prosperity, have to learn that by exploiting the natural world they have jeopardized the future of the earth on which we all depend. They now need to learn again from the Indigenous peoples whose ways they often regarded as backward and whom they often considered obstacles to technological and economic advance. Age-old Indigenous wisdom about how to treat the earth gently and manage its resources in a sustainable way is now urgently needed by the entire global community.

Christian discipleship in today's context calls for a vision of faith that embraces the earth itself. As the *Cape Town Commitment* states,

> If Jesus is Lord of all the earth, we cannot separate our relationship to Christ from how we act in relation to the earth. For to proclaim the gospel that says "Jesus is Lord" is to proclaim the gospel that includes the earth, since Christ's Lordship is over all creation. Creation care is a thus a gospel issue within the Lordship of Christ. *Such love for God's creation* demands that we repent of our part in the destruction, waste and pollution of the earth's resources and our collusion in the toxic idolatry of consumerism. Instead, we commit ourselves to urgent and prophetic ecological responsibility.[109]

"The Arusha Report" underlines the sacrificial commitment that this entails: "If evangelism is to bring good news today, it needs to entail the *kenosis* that puts the long-term sustainability of the earth ahead of our own short-term comfort and convenience."[110] Such a commitment is driven by a vision of the salvation that God has revealed in Jesus Christ:

> For the creation was subjected to futility, not of its own will but by the will of the one who subjected it, in hope that the creation itself will be set free from its bondage

---

108. "The Arusha Conference Report," 11.

109. *Cape Town Commitment,* §I 7.

110. "The Arusha Conference Report," 11.

to decay and will obtain the freedom of the glory of the children of God. We know that the whole creation has been groaning in labor pains until now (Rom. 8:20-22)

This is an awareness that must be close to the heart of anyone concerned with mission and discipleship today.

Questions for Reflection

Can you give examples of how climate change is affecting our world?

Why are some nations affected more than others by climate change?

What does it mean to care for God's creation by the way we live our lives?

7. BELONGING TOGETHER

We are called as disciples to belong together in just and inclusive communities, in our quest for unity and on our ecumenical journey, in a world that is based upon marginalization and exclusion.

Belonging Together

The composition of the Conference on World Mission and Evangelism in Arusha was marked by extraordinary diversity. As "The Arusha Conference Report" notes,

> With its broad participation from Protestant, Orthodox, Roman Catholic, Evangelical, Pentecostal, and African Instituted churches, the conference showed that the nature and character of mission and evangelism is truly multi-directional and multi-faceted. It indicated that there is not one centre but many centres impacting, shaping, and informing the understanding and practice of mission and evangelism in our time. Those present in Arusha were people from many parts of the world and of different ages, cultures, experiences, perspectives, and orientations, each with stories of suffering and struggle as well as of hope and determination, celebrating the richness of the diversity of God's creation.[111]

Yet this most diverse of gatherings was marked by a passionate and committed sense of belonging together, united by a shared response to Jesus' call to discipleship. The Arusha Call is the expression of this unity.

At first sight, to talk of discipleship might seem to involve a turn to the individual. Each must hear the call to discipleship for themselves and embark on their own personal journey. However, no one travels far on this journey without discovering that they have fellow-travellers. More than that – the journey is one that draws them ever closer to their fellow disciples. As Anthony Gittins remarks, "*Disciple* is not a self-defining word and does not identify a totally self-sufficient person, for no disciple is an independent agent. Disciples are interdependent, first in relation to Jesus and then in relation to each other. They form a community, united in faith and mission, if

---

111. "The Arusha Conference Report," 5.

not in a specific locality."[112] As the then WCC General Secretary Olav Fykse Tveit told the Arusha conference: "The mission of God in following Jesus Christ and his example is always pointing to the other, to those who are around us. The calling is about focusing on them – not us . . . Disciples are not called to be alone."[113]

A commitment to discipleship is both deeply personal and thoroughly communal. Hence, the Arusha conference took note:

> In a world that prizes individuality, at a time when society is increasingly atomized, and in a context where people are polarized by identity politics, Christ calls his disciples to community. Following him means moving away from a self-centred life to find fulfillment in generous self-giving – the way of Christ. The journey is one that transforms and shapes the lives of others; a journey not to be made alone, but together. Discipleship is not only vertical but also horizontal in its scope and expression.[114]

The transformation entailed in discipleship is one that opens us up to others in ways we might never have imagined. As Kirsteen Kim comments, "Discipleship is more than individual formation; it is 'joining in' with what the Holy Spirit is doing in the lives of others."[115]

The commitment to belong together is being urged at a time when the landscape of global Christianity is rapidly changing. There are large-scale expressions of Christian faith that barely existed when the ecumenical movement began in 1910. In this context, a new dividing line may engage ecumenical energy: the difference in ethos between Western and Southern Christianity. Philip Jenkins has pointed out, "Southern Christianity, the Third Church, is not just a transplanted version of the familiar religion of the older Christian states: the New Christendom is no mirror image of the Old. It is a truly new and developing entity. Just how different from its predecessor remains to be seen."[116]

Debates in several global ecclesial communions over human sexuality have revealed something of the extent of the potential differences. Moreover, while

---

112. Anthony J. Gittins, *The Way of Discipleship: Women, Men and Today's Call to Mission* (Collegeville: Liturgical Press, 2016), 41.

113. Tveit, "Opening Address," 54.

114. "The Arusha Conference Report," 14.

115. Kim, "Mission after the Arusha Conference," 418.

116. Philip Jenkins, *The Next Christendom: The Coming of Global Christianity* (Oxford: Oxford University Press, 2002), 214.

sexuality is the presenting issue, the debate clearly rests on deeper issues of authority: Who sets the standards in doctrinal and ethical matters? The challenge of numerous and vibrant Southern Christians to the assumptions and premises of "Old Christendom" brings a new frontier to the ecumenical landscape. Will Christianity fragment into a variety of Christianities that scarcely recognize one another? Or will a new ecumenism find ways to celebrate diversity while affirming unity in inspiring and energizing ways? American China specialist Philip Wickeri suggests, "Those of us from the historic Protestant churches need to be in dialogue with popular Christianity, both to share our understanding of the gospel with each other, and also to better understand and learn from the spirit which moves new Christian communities."[117] When we commit to belonging together it means reaching across deep divides created by culture, history, and ecclesiology (way of being church).

Without such commitment, our discipleship is liable to remain shallow or even become self-indulgent. Such shared commitment is counter-cultural, but it is the path of discipleship. For Christ's disciples, nurturing community is a key part of their calling. The Arusha conference found,

> In individualized societies, the perception of what is important and what is true is being shaped increasingly by personal experience instead of a transfer of tradition, knowledge, and facts. Therefore, the church must find ways to let people experience the importance and meaning of being disciples together. Of great importance are baptism and eucharist, both reminding people that they are part of the movement of God's Spirit in this world. Elites, distances and divisions based on social constructs of power and privilege have no place in the community that God wants to create.[118]

Marginalization and Exclusion

The Arusha conference was well aware that it was making its call in a world that is based on marginalization and exclusion. Far from making for community, the forces shaping the global economy are driving people apart. Resources are concentrated at the centre for the benefit of the few, while more and more people find themselves marginalized and excluded. It has become commonplace that power and resources are being concentrated in the hands of the 1 percent, with the corollary that large numbers find themselves marginalized and excluded. This raises a

---

117. Philip L. Wickeri, "Mission from the Margins: The Missio Dei in the Crisis of World Christianity," *International Review of Mission* 93 (April 2004), 182–98, at 195.

118. "The Arusha Conference Report," 14–15.

whole range of issues for the human community and is manifestly unsustainable. The work of Thomas Piketty has demonstrated that national economies are imperilled by excessive inequality.[119] For the churches, the question is even more acute: What does it mean to belong together when such powerful forces drive us apart? How can we speak meaningfully of the oneness of the church when some members enjoy life among the comfortable elite while others suffer extremes of privation and exclusion?

Awareness of climate change has thrown the obscene inequality that prevails in the global economy into yet sharper relief. It is not the wealthy but rather the poor who suffer the immediate negative effects of global warming, as poverty often includes being forced to live on marginal land that is vulnerable to natural disasters. By and large, the world's poorest communities have made the least contribution to causing global warming. Yet it is they who are already struggling to feed their families as a result of climate change. It is in the interests of everyone to act to counter global warming, but those who have the cause of the poor at heart have an added imperative. Action on climate change must be allied with efforts to resolve the debt crisis, create just trade rules, and increase well-targeted aid if real hope of defeating poverty is to be within reach for the 2.8 billion people who are living on less than two dollars a day.

Called to profess and enact the oneness of the church across deep social, economic, and environmental division, the churches have a mandate to speak out for justice. This is not a matter of armchair observation. Rather, prophetic critique is forged through solidarity on the ground. Since the World Bank's Voices of the Poor project of the late 1990s, recognition has grown that "faith-based organizations" play a vital role in combating poverty in the global South. Many, against all the odds, have continued to offer hope, to provide health and educational services, and to promote development in some of the least resourced communities in the world. Highly funded and highly acclaimed donor-driven development projects have come and gone, often with little to show at the end of the day. Meanwhile, the churches continue, from a meagre resource base, to provide essential social services and to inspire fresh initiatives in development within the poor communities they serve. Such action,

---

119. See Thomas Piketty, *Capital in the Twenty-first Century* (Boston: Harvard University Press, 2014).

which finds organizational expression today in the ACT Alliance,[120] is indispensable to the integrity of disciples who claim to belong together.

The potential significance of the churches' role should not be underestimated. Sojourners leader Jim Wallis has stated,

> For the first time in history we have the information, knowledge, technology, and resources to bring the worst of global poverty to an end. What we don't have is the moral and political will to do so. And it is becoming clear that it will take a new moral energy to create the political will. I believe the religious communities of the world could provide the "tipping point" in the struggle to eliminate the world's most extreme poverty. Faith communities could provide the crucial social leadership the world desperately needs, and I don't see where else that prophetic leadership might come from.[121]

With their eschatological imagination, the churches are uniquely well-placed to sustain the conviction that "another world is possible." When others flag or become disillusioned by apparently immovable resistance to positive change, the churches are energized by faith in the promise that the purpose of God revealed in Jesus Christ will ultimately find expression in the new world God will bring to birth. The commitment to "belong together" provides another powerful motivator when it comes to combating marginalization and exclusion.

To be a disciple of Christ today involves a critical stance in relation to the exclusionary dynamics of the global economy. Prophetic critique can be raised in various ways, but perhaps the most powerful will be the formation of communities that demonstrate a very different model.

Just and Inclusive Communities

Given the forces of marginalization and exclusion that are shaping the life and experience of many, the Arusha Call's summons to "belong together" represents a radical option – the more so when it explains that this is not just a matter of superficial unity but rather of forming just and inclusive communities. In doing so, the Call responds to a yearning that is deeply felt in our time. As Wesley Granberg-Michaelson has observed,

120. ACT Alliance is a coalition of 151 churches and faith-based organizations working together in over 125 countries; see https://actalliance.org.

121. Jim Wallis, *God's Politics: Why the American Right Gets It Wrong and the Left Doesn't Get It* (Oxford: Lion, 2005), 270.

> Technological, economic, and social innovation sweeping the globe are producing two irreversible changes throughout world Christianity. First, adherents of faith have less trust and loyalty toward established religious institutions, especially as they attempt to determine for their followers patterns of belief and religious practices to guide their daily lives. Second, participation in local Christian congregations and groups is being driven more by the experience of belonging to a welcoming, nurturing community than by doctrinal agreement and dogmatic belief.[122]

Likewise, Robert Webber, in his book *Ancient-Future Faith*, argues that the most significant apologetic Christians will be able to offer in this century is the quality of life and welcome within the church. A community that embodies the experience of the kingdom will draw people to itself. He says, "In this sense the church and its life in the world will become the new apologetic. People come to faith not because they see the logic of the argument, but because they have experienced a welcoming God in a hospitable and loving community."[123] In order to be such a convincing community, the church will need to be characterized by both justice and inclusion.

This calls for a church that is alert to injustice and exclusion. In its own life and practice, the church needs to be actively countering historic injustice and promoting the inclusion of those who, for whatever reason, have tended to be excluded. It also needs to be counter-cultural and intentional in fostering community identity. When it came to the Arusha conference itself, the Ecumenical Disability Network (EDAN) played an important role, bringing from their pre-conference meeting a deep concern for inclusion and an understanding that moving in the Spirit involves sensitivity to those who are not yet included. The Arusha conference encouraged overcoming cultures and practices of discrimination and exclusion that deny the dignity and rights of others, holding this as an important indicator of the work of the Spirit,

> Too often, churches have been comfortable clubs for "people like us" and have been easily abused to assert the interests of one identity set against others. Today we urgently need churches that break down the dividing walls of hostility and practise radical hospitality, living out the reconciliation and unity promised by Christ and forged by the Spirit. Too often, churches have been inward looking and preoccupied with their own internal concerns. Today we urgently need churches that are mainly and foremost churches in mission – agents of the Spirit in the transformation of the

---

122. Granberg-Michaelson, *Future Faith*, 212.

123. Robert Webber, *Ancient-Future Faith* (Grand Rapids: Baker Books, 1999), 72; cited in Christine D. Pohl, "Biblical Issues in Mission and Migration," *Missiology: An International Review* 31:1 (2003), 12.

world. All of this calls for formation, an intentional journey of becoming disciples together.[124]

Our Ecumenical Journey

In 1948, when the WCC held its first assembly in Amsterdam, its members committed to stay together. When they met for the 10th Assembly in Busan in 2013, they committed to journey together, a commitment that took the form of a "Pilgrimage of Justice and Peace." In choosing this theme as a defining motif for its journey in the early 21st century, the WCC, in the words of its Faith and Order Commission, "has not only affirmed the desire to move together, but also it affirms that it is a movement directed toward the reign of God, that it is a transformative way of faith and life, and that it is a journey which churches take together with other companions and in the context of the whole world."[125]

The Arusha conference was aware of how deeply intertwined are mission and unity. In a divided and polarized world, mission is compelling when it is a matter of unity. In his "Director's Report" to the Arusha conference, Jooseop Keum observed,

> The world is broken. Therefore, it is imperative for the ecumenical movement to boldly witness the unity in the triune God and to live it out for the unity of humanity. The world is yearning for a Christian discipleship which reconciles the broken and troubled world. In order to do so, unity of the church and mission is not an optional agenda.[126]

There is no discipleship without community. To be a disciple is to be on a journey away from a self-centred life and toward a life of generous self-giving – the way of Christ. This creates community with those who are walking the same journey. One of the preparatory papers for the Arusha conference stated, "The fruit of the Spirit – love, joy, peace, patience, kindness, goodness, faith, gentleness, self-control – finds expression in the context of community. There is much to learn from African communities that put a premium on

---

124. "The Arusha Conference Report," 15.

125. *Come and See: A Theological Invitation to the Pilgrimage of Justice and Peace*, Faith and Order Paper No. 224 (Geneva: WCC, 2019), 26–27.

126. Jooseop Keum, "CWME: From Athens to Arusha – Director's Report," in Jukko and Keum, eds., *Moving in the Spirit*, 73–87, at 86.

the relational dimension of life."[127] A World Mission Conference that met in Africa was convinced we are called to belong together in just and inclusive communities.

Questions for Reflection

Who are the people missing at our table? Whom do we need to include in our Christian communities? Whom have we excluded?

What forces can you identify that marginalize and exclude?

What might be your next steps on "our ecumenical journey"?

---

127. CWME Study Document "Together on the Path: Called to Transforming Discipleship," in Risto Jukko, ed., *Conference on World Mission and Evangelism, 2018. Complete Digital Edition of the Arusha Report*, 232–42, at 238, https://www.oikoumene.org/en/resources/publications/DigitalEdition_ArushaReport_ALL.pdf.

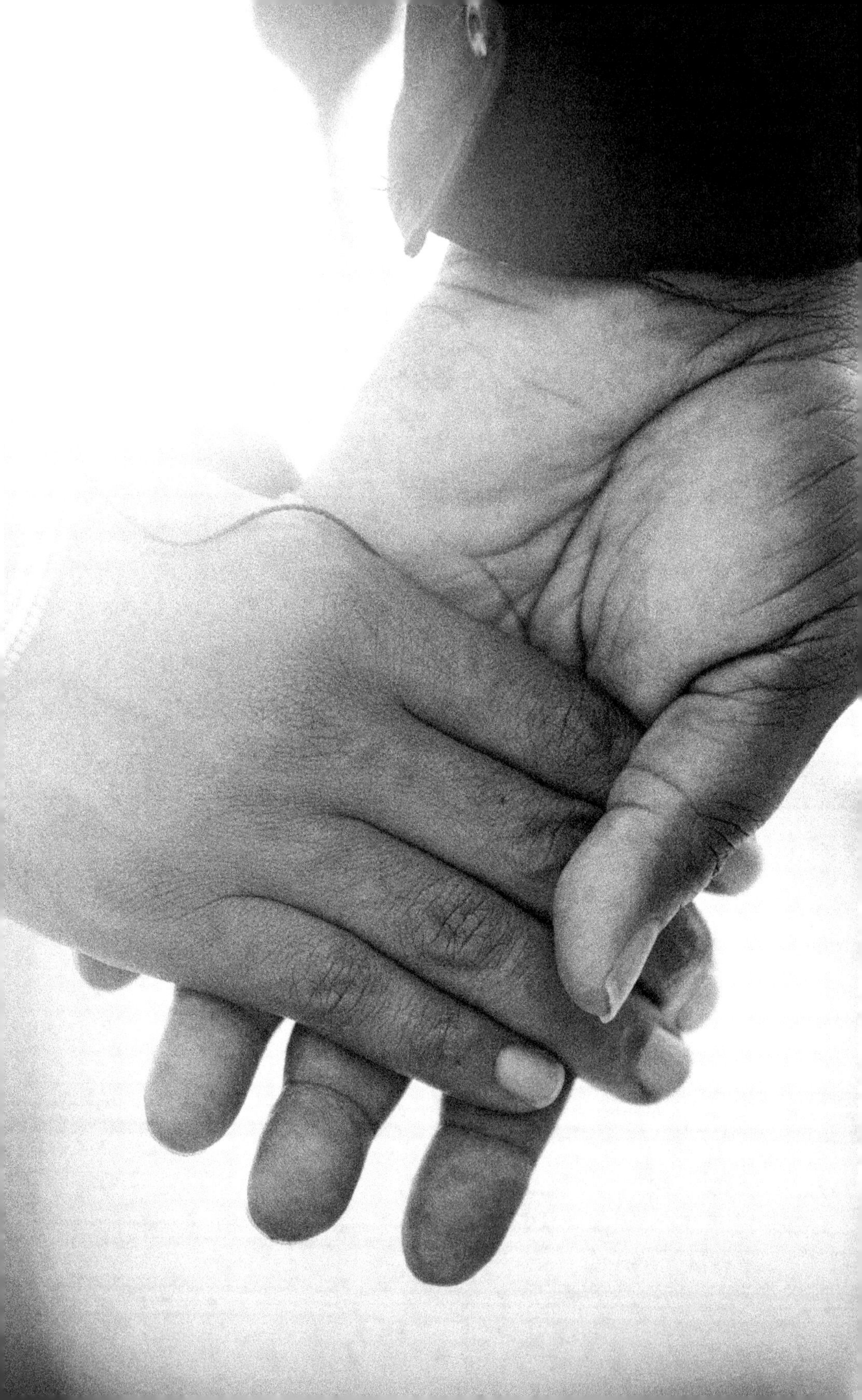

8. PEOPLE OF OTHER FAITHS

We are called to be faithful witnesses of God's transforming love in dialogue with people of other faiths in a world where the politicization of religious identities often causes conflict.

People of Other Faiths

The question of relations with people of other faiths has a long history in the sequence of World Mission conferences that led to the one at Arusha. It was a focal point of discussion at the first in the series, held at Edinburgh in 1910, which devoted one of its eight preparatory commissions to the question of "The missionary message in relation to non-Christian religions." Of all the commission reports this was the most original and attracts the greatest interest today. It is remarkable for the degree to which it scotches the idea that Western missionaries were iconoclasts bent on the eradication of existing religions to impose their own understanding of Christianity. On the contrary, the report consistently argues that the appropriate attitude of the Christian missionary to the non-Christian religions is one of sympathetic understanding. It was guided by a fulfilment theology that regarded Christianity as the fulfilment of the other religions. While today this would be regarded as patronizing and triumphalist, at the time it aimed to provide for an irenic Christian encounter with people adhering to non-Christian religions, which would present the gospel as the fulfilment of their own inner hopes and yearnings.

The question remained high on the agenda of the missionary movement and found a particular focus when the third World Mission Conference was held in the religiously plural context of India in 1938. The conference was held at Tambaram, near Chennai (Madras), and an important part of the preparation was a commission to the Dutch missiologist Hendrik Kraemer to "state the fundamental position of the Christian church as a witness-bearing body in the modern world, relating this to conflicting views of the attitude to be taken by Christians towards other faiths and dealing in detail with the evangelistic approach to the great non-Christian faiths."[128] The result was a full-length book entitled *The Christian Message in a Non-Christian World.* [129]

The church, Kraemer argued, draws its true identity "from the apostolic urgency of gladly witnessing to God and his saving and redeeming Power through Christ."[130] He expressed strong suspicion of any notion that the kingdom of God would come through human effort, stressing instead the divine initiative. Nor could Christianity, in Kraemer's view, be regarded as the fulfilment of other religions. Rather, a dialectical approach was required in which the presence and action of God in other religious traditions could be affirmed but where this would always be seen in the light of the unexpectedness and "discontinuity" of God's decisive action in Jesus Christ. If missionaries lacked the confidence that Jesus was "the Way, the Truth, and the Life," how would they be able to call men and women to costly conversion?

A century later, the question of the place of other faiths in the purposes of God remains centre stage. The global context, however, has changed markedly. A hundred years ago, missionaries had great confidence in the superiority of Christianity as a religion and expected that the other ancient religions would fade away in the face of the Christian advance. Today, by contrast, it is apparent that all faiths have been renewing their life and mission. Contrary to the expectations of earlier secularization theory, the advent of modernity has not, in much of the world, been accompanied by the abandonment of religion. In fact, many people have become more fervent and devoted in their faith – so much so that religious fervour often spills over into violent aggression against the adherents of another faith. As Hans Küng has famously argued, if there is to be peace among the nations there must first be peace among the religions.[131]

The Arusha conference was very much aware of the peace imperative. Its challenge was how to balance or integrate this with the mandate for world mission and evangelism. It was "impressed by the mutual respect and ease of interaction between different religious communities that prevails in many parts of Africa (and beyond). With sharp challenges to face at personal, communal, and national levels, in many contexts Christians have been creative in finding ways to work together across religious boundaries."[132] A key

---

128. IMC Ad Interim Committee Minutes (Old Jordans, 1936), cited in Timothy Yates, *Christian Mission in the Twentieth Century* (Cambridge: Cambridge University Press, 1994), 108.

129. Hendrik Kraemer, *The Christian Message in a Non-Christian World* (London: Edinburgh House Press, 1938).

130. Ibid., vi.

131. See e.g. Hans Küng, *Christianity, Essence, History, Future* (London: Continuum, 1996).

132. "The Arusha Conference Report," 13.

question was how to foster harmonious relations between different religious communities while at the same time upholding the integrity of mission and evangelism.

Religion and Politics

Few would dispute the observation that religious identity is often a factor in situations of conflict and violence. The different sides in the long-running conflict in the Middle East are often defined by religious allegiance. The fault line between Christians and Muslims in many parts of the world is one that gives rise to conflict and warfare. Violence based on religious identity has assumed such proportions as to amount to war crimes or even genocide. The Daesh genocide against religious minorities in Syria and Iraq and the Myanmar government's genocide against Rohingya Muslims in Rakhine State are two of the more egregious examples in recent times. Meanwhile, in the minds of those targeted, the violence and destruction perpetrated by Western countries are often associated with the Christian faith that has long shaped their culture and society.[133]

As a result of these realities of the early 21st century, the salience of religion in many conflict situations around the world has been, for many, an unexpected development. American scholar Philip Jenkins has commented, "However much this would have surprized political analysts a generation or two ago, the critical political frontiers around the world are decided not by attitudes toward class or dialectical materialism, but by rival concepts of God."[134] The ideological role played by religion in situations of conflict can very quickly subvert the imperative for peace and reconciliation that lies at the heart of biblical faith. If Christian mission is not able to function credibly as a force for peace and reconciliation, then its claims are soon going to look hollow.

The reason Christian faith too often finds itself being deployed as an ideological prop for aggression and violence is that it is vulnerable to being co-opted by political forces that have their own agenda to pursue. This is what the Arusha Call has in its sights when it speaks of the politicization of religious identity often causing conflict. Too often, religious communities have allowed themselves to be pawns in a game being played by political masters to the extent that their own core purpose is subverted and their identity

---

133. See further R. Scott Appleby, *The Ambivalence of the Sacred: Religion, Violence and Reconciliation* (Lanham and Oxford: Rowman and Littlefield, 2000).

134. Jenkins, *The Next Christendom*, 163.

distorted. Political advantage can often be gained by pitting one community against another. Since communities are often defined by their religious loyalties, religious identity can easily come to define a conflict that has been stirred up in pursuit of a political project. The Arusha conference suggested that the path of discipleship leads in a different direction. It sought to expose the captivity of religious identity by political projects and called Christians to be pro-active in resisting such co-option by taking a different direction, one that is directly inspired by their faith.

Witness and Dialogue

When we ask how our faith shapes our relations with those belonging to other faiths, the challenge for proponents of Christian mission is how to hold in balance the peace imperative and the evangelistic imperative. Clearly, both have deep roots in the biblical faith. Jesus *both* blessed the peacemakers *and* commanded his followers to proclaim the good news to all nations. Many Christians have opted to give priority to either one emphasis or the other to the extent that this has become one of the most divisive questions in the churches today. The time has come to confront this polarity. In order to properly understanding core features of Christian belief – such as the Trinity, the uniqueness of Jesus Christ, salvation, and conversion – we need to consider these in light of the plurality of religions. A host of practical questions also arise around evangelism, proselytization, dialogue, and encounter.

The "Edinburgh 2010 Common Call" sought to balance the two mandates that are inherent in the faith:

> Remembering Christ's sacrifice on the Cross and his resurrection for the world's salvation, and empowered by the Holy Spirit, we are called to authentic dialogue, respectful engagement and humble witness among people of other faiths – and no faith – to the uniqueness of Christ. Our approach is marked with bold confidence in the gospel message; it builds friendship, seeks reconciliation and practises hospitality.[135]

The following year, a promising new direction for interreligious relations was charted by a joint statement of the WCC, the Pontifical Council for Interreligious Dialogue, and the World Evangelical Alliance:

---

135. "Edinburgh 2010 Common Call," §2, in Kim and Anderson, *Edinburgh 2010*, 1.

Aware of tensions between people and communities of different religious convictions and varied interpretations of Christian witness, authentic evangelism must always be guided by life-affirming values, as stated in the joint statement on "Christian Witness in a Multi-Religious World: Recommendations for Conduct":

a. Rejection of all forms of violence, discrimination and repression by religious and secular authority, including the abuse of power – psychological or social.

b. Affirming the freedom of religion to practice and profess faith without any fear of reprisal and or intimidation. Mutual respect and solidarity which promote justice, peace and the common good of all.

c. Respect for all people and human cultures, while also discerning the elements in our own cultures, such as patriarchy, racism, casteism, etc., that need to be challenged by the gospel.

d. Renunciation of false witness and listening in order to understand in mutual respect.

e. Ensuring freedom for ongoing discernment by persons and communities as part of decision-making.

f. Building relationships with believers of other faiths or no faith to facilitate deeper mutual understanding, reconciliation and cooperation for the common good.[136]

Heart-searching and integrity are thus needed on the part of those who engage with people of other faiths in their missionary calling. As Peniel Rajkumar explains, "The challenge for proponents of mission and dialogue is to carry out their respective agendas... employing an epistemology which does not denigrate the marginalized as merely 'objects' of their agenda and understands conversion within a wider intersection of religious freedom, human dignity, economic and political interests, and social privilege and power."[137]

Together towards Life took this approach further with its orientation to the Holy Spirit, opening up new space in which to acknowledge the presence and integrity of other faiths:

In the plurality and complexity of today's world, we encounter people of many different faiths, ideologies, and convictions. We believe that the Spirit of Life brings joy and fullness of life. God's Spirit, therefore, can be found in all cultures that affirm

---

136. WCC, Pontifical Council for Interreligious Dialogue, and the World Evangelical Alliance, "Christian Witness in a Multi-Religious World (2011)," cited in *Together towards Life*, §90.

137. Peniel Rajkumar, "Other Faiths," in Ross et al., *Ecumenical Missiology*, 218–34, at 232.

life. The Holy Spirit works in mysterious ways and we do not fully understand the workings of the Spirit in other faith traditions. We acknowledge that there is inherent value and wisdom in diverse life-giving spiritualities. Therefore, authentic mission makes the "other" a partner in, not an "object" of mission.[138]

A major WCC Faith and Order paper on the church published in the same year as *Together towards Life* sought to strike a similar balance between openness to others and confidence in the gospel: "Today Christians are more aware of the wide array of different religions other than their own and of the positive truths and values they contain . . . Sharing the joyful news of the truth revealed in the New Testament and inviting others to the fullness of life in Christ is an expression of respectful love."[139]

The Arusha conference built on this openness to the other, with acute sensitivity to the issues of religion and conflict that have been so prominent in the early 21st century. Guided by this concern, the conference charted a fresh direction for interfaith relations:

> A comprehensive orientation to the mission of God calls for a welcoming and hospitable way of life that is affirmative and bridge building. People of other faiths are to be welcomed in the process of learning and formation. Interreligious encounters and the mutual learning they offer need to be a part of missional formation. Therefore, theological education and congregational learning processes need to be implemented in a manner that enables an integrated interreligious participation without compromising Christian identity.[140]

At the Arusha conference, Kathryn Mary Lohre, a Lutheran theologian from the United States, went further:

> There is a unique role . . . for the churches to play. We are just beginning to understand that equipping disciples for mission and evangelism today must include not only religious literacy and interreligious competencies, but also the courage and humility to embrace the cross for the sake of our neighbours of other religions and world views, and to defend them against discrimination, bigotry, racism, and violence, regardless of its source.[141]

---

138. *Together towards Life,* §93.

139. *The Church: Towards a Common Vision,* Faith and Order Paper No. 214 (Geneva: WCC, 2013), 60.

140. "The Arusha Conference Report," 13.

141. Kathryn Mary Lohre, "Carrying the Cross of Prejudice from a Dominant Culture," in Jukko and Keum, eds., *Moving in the Spirit,* 156–59, at 157.

A solidarity that is not about the interests of our own religious community but rather about embracing others who are under threat might be the witness for which our world is waiting.

God's Transforming Love

The Arusha Call frames its consideration of relations with people of other faiths within the overarching need to witness to God's transforming love. This puts interreligious relations in perspective. Lamin Sanneh has said, "For all of us pluralism can be a rock of stumbling but for God it is the cornerstone of universal design."[142] This points to the humility that allows our own understanding to be relativized in relation to God's sovereignty and majesty. This need not involve an abandonment of confidence in the biblical message.

The San Antonio mission conference of 1989 stated, "We cannot point to any other way of salvation than Jesus Christ; at the same time we cannot set limits to the saving power of God."[143] This careful balance of confidence and provisionality is echoed in the 2019 Faith and Order paper on the Pilgrimage of Justice and Peace: "[Christians] can share the riches of the Christian faith without making judgements which belong to God alone."[144]

The Arusha Call's sensitivity to the need for both respectful dialogue and faithful witness to the love of God opens up a space that invites more attention as Christians seek to be champions of peace while at the same time remaining true to their faith. Peniel Rajkumar suggests where this might lead: "Pneumatology and Christology will be two issues that will push mission theology to widen the horizons of its imaginations critically and creatively so that our witness to the hope that is within us in a pluralistic world is both compassionately Christian and passionately interreligious. This demands theological integrity and interreligious sensitivity."[145] The Arusha Call embodies a strong sense that both of these are needed, never one at the expense of the other.

---

142. Lamin Sanneh, *Translating the Message: The Missionary Impact on Culture* (Maryknoll: Orbis Books, 1989), 29.

143. San Antonio, Section 1 report, paragraph 26.

144. *Come and See*, 25.

145. Rajkumar, "Other Faiths," 229.

Questions for Reflection

Can you give examples of situations where politicization of religious identities causes conflict?

How can we be both faithful witnesses and in dialogue with people of other faiths?

Do you know any women and men from other religions? What is your experience with them?

9. SERVANT LEADERS

We are called to be formed as servant leaders who demonstrate the way of Christ in a world that privileges power, wealth, and the culture of money (Luke 22:25–27).

Formation as Disciples

To be a disciple is to be in process of formation. It is a matter of taking raw material and forming it into something with distinctive shape and purpose. A disciple is one who is learning from a master and being shaped by that learning. For followers of Jesus, Christ is their master and their life is reshaped and transformed through their experience of knowing him and walking on the path along which he leads. Surveying a century of ecumenical thinking about the meaning of discipleship, Benjamin Conner observes, "However discipleship has been conceived in the ecumenical movement, it has always indicated the importance of shaping and forming *people* to be and do certain things in response to the missionary calling of a missionary God."[146]

One important thrust of the Arusha Call was its recognition that leadership is a key question in today's world. What is leadership? What kind of leadership does our world need? What kind of leadership are the churches called to offer? In line with its central theme, the Arusha Call sets the question of leadership in the context of discipleship. As Knud Jørgensen observed, "The person, who has not learned to be a disciple, cannot be a leader."[147]

During the second half of the 20th century, ecumenical thinking about discipleship led to an emphasis on life and service in the world. Rather than thinking narrowly about living the life of faith within the framework of the church, we began to think of discipleship in context of the broader canvas of the purposes of God in the world at large. Much was beneficial about this turn to the world, but it carried the risk that a life of service in the wider world might become detached from the roots of the life of discipleship in the worshipping life of the church. For the sake of formation, it is important to strike the right balance between church and world:

---

146. Benjamin Conner, "Discipleship," in Ross et al., *Ecumenical Missiology*, 246–58, at 247.

147. Jørgensen, *Equipping for Service*, 35.

> The ecumenical concept of discipleship that had moved out of religion and into history is now returning to the church . . . The turn back to the church is for the sake of strengthening disciples through faithful Christian practices, and the turn represents the recognition that immersion in the world without the guidance of the church has often led to "malformation".[148]

The path of discipleship leads to faithful and committed service in the world at large, yet the disciple still needs to be equipped and refreshed by remaining well-grounded in the life and worship of the church.

When we think of formation, we think also of the formal and academic settings where people are prepared for life and leadership. Here too the call to discipleship needs to be heard. As it was stated in one of the preparatory documents for the Arusha conference,

> The comprehensive nature of the call to discipleship brings a challenge also to theological education. Even in academic work the vision of transforming discipleship cannot be reduced to a merely intellectual exercise. Intellectual rigour and the highest academic standards must be applied to developing a curriculum that invites us to personal engagement that is life-giving. Academic rigour contributes to a formation that is comprehensive in reaching the roots of our being and the depths of our contemporary crisis. Those who hear the call to the journey of transformed discipleship need to be ready to participate in a transformative journey in the power of the Spirit as the distinctive notes of Christian discipleship strike chords in hearts and minds.[149]

Richard Rohr has suggested that Christians do not think their way into a new life; they live their way into a new kind of thinking.[150] Discipleship involves taking the option to adopt a distinctive way of life; it is through living that life that a new epistemological framework is constructed. The pressures of academic recognition and accreditation must not be allowed to inhibit a formation that produces not only degree-holders but disciples.

A Rival Formation

As the Arusha Call sets a vision of being formed as servant leaders it does so with full awareness that this is not the only call to formation that will

---

148. Conner, "Discipleship," 257–58.

149. "Together on the Path: Called to Transforming Discipleship," 233.

150. Richard Rohr, "Belief or Discipleship," Center for Action and Contemplation, 22 January 2019, https://cac.org/belief-or-discipleship-2019-01-22/.

be heard in today's world. In fact, a widely prevalent formation exists that would take us in a very different direction. The "global system of mammon," which *Together towards Life* sought to expose, is also in the business of formation. In fact, to resist the global system of mammon will involve determined swimming against the tide. Wesley Granberg-Michaelson remarks, "Money is the idol operative in most of our lives, controlling many of the decisions we make, permeating our values, and motivating many of our actions. Achieving freedom from the dominating power of money in our lives requires hard work in our souls."[151] The Arusha conference was ready for such hard work.

The conference report states,

> In today's global context, there is a formation that presents a sharp challenge to Christian discipleship. The culture of money seeks to define and dominate every aspect of human activity and every creature of God's world. It forms possessor-consumers to be compliant constituents of an economically constructed world. This formation influences both thought and behaviour. Capturing individuals and communities, it aspires to draw a comprehensive map of our human and ecological future. The human soul and human community are stunted by the institutionalization and amplification of greed in an unrestrained market society. The integrity and well-being of creation is directly and dangerously threatened. We must engage in a determined attempt to present, for this generation, a faithful alternative to the spiritual formation offered by the culture of money.[152]

Besides exposing destructive patterns of leadership in the world at large, we can bring a prophetic critique to bear on the church itself: "Too often, the church has been moulded by prevailing patterns of the surrounding world, its leaders seeking power and wealth for themselves rather than modelling the sacrificial service seen in Christ. Today we urgently need church leaders who are, first and foremost, disciples, walking in the Spirit, forming and guiding communities that take the way of Jesus."[153]

---

151. Wesley Granberg-Michaelson, *Leadership from Inside Out: Spirituality and Organizational Change* (New York: Crossroad, 2004), 18.

152. "The Arusha Conference Report," 16.

153. Ibid., 15.

Servant Leaders

Surveying the global context in the early 21st century, Doug Birdsall, former executive chair of the Lausanne Movement, arrived at the following conclusion: "I am increasingly convinced that the greatest needs are not about new strategies and programs, nor are they about better buildings, more personnel, additional financial resources, and innovative use of technology, as important as these issues are. No, the greatest need is for leaders, men and women with Christ-like character, faith, and vision."[154]

The Arusha conference advanced a clear idea of the qualities required of leaders:

> This vision of discipleship is geared to the formation of leaders who are equipped not only intellectually, but particularly at the level of spiritual discernment and personal transformation. It fosters a radical openness to the Spirit of God that finds expression in leadership marked by mutuality, reciprocity, humility, and interdependence. It provokes a radical openness to others that is life-affirming and profound in its integrity. This openness and humility have clear implications: respect, rights, and dignity are not denied on the bases of the cultures of domination, discrimination, and exclusion.[155]

In the opening plenary of the Arusha conference, Mutale Mulenga-Kaunda set the tone:

> The kind of resistance needed in the struggle against the life-denying forces requires that the followers of Jesus Christ are filled with the life-giving Spirit of God that alone can equip people with the necessary resources for transformative discipleship . . . Disciples are formed through a process of belonging, believing, becoming, and participating in order to live out the mission of God as demonstrated through Christ's mission in the church.[156]

To become a servant leader one must be ready to swim against the tide, one must be intentional in opting for a way of life different from the prevailing norm. As noted in conference report, "A spirituality of resilience is

---

154. S. Douglas Birdsall, "Foreword," in Knud Jørgensen, *Equipping for Service: Christian Leadership in Church and Society* (Oxford: Regnum, 2012), x.

155. "The Arusha Conference Report," 16.

156. Mutale Mulenga-Kaunda, "Young African Women and the Search for a Liberated Future," in Jukko and Keum, eds., *Moving in the Spirit*, 65–72, at 68.

at the centre of the theological and missional formation for discipleship. It requires the formation of communities of Christians that are resilient in the face of injustice, that are humble and courageous in persistently challenging the unjust system."[157]

The Way of Christ

An earlier WCC Conference on World Mission and Evangelism, held at San Antonio in 1989, coined the phrase, "mission in Christ's way."[158] At a time when many questions were being asked about the validity of mission, one convincing answer was to think of it in terms of following in the way of Christ. This was echoed in The Arusha Call to Discipleship almost 30 years later. When we take this as our cue, we find that it points us in the direction of servant leadership. This is a major theme of the gospel, powerfully expressed, for example, in Luke 22:25–27:

> But he said to them, "The kings of the Gentiles lord it over them; and those in authority over them are called benefactors. But not so with you; rather the greatest among you must become like the youngest, and the leader like one who serves. For who is greater, the one who is at the table or the one who serves? Is it not the one at the table? But I am among you as one who serves."

Reflecting on this pattern, the Arusha conference found the following:

> Transforming discipleship in the spirit of mission from the margins creates for us a possibility to reset the ways in which we exercise power, share leadership, and organize our partnerships in mission. As leaders, it is important for us to grasp that we must disciple in the context of relationship. One reason Jesus had such a lasting impact on his disciples is that he lived his message before them daily. He was both message and method. By walking with Jesus, they saw how he lived his faith in the real world. He prayed before them. He fed the poor. He had compassion on the multitudes. He healed the sick. In other words, he lived the life that he wanted to reproduce in his disciples.[159]

---

157. "The Arusha Conference Report," 16.

158. Frederick R. Wilson, ed., *The San Antonio Report. Your Will Be Done: Mission in Christ's Way* (Geneva: WCC Publications, 1990).

159. "The Arusha Conference Report," 15–16.

The leadership that is needed today depends on faithfulness in discipleship, in a close and committed following of Jesus Christ.

We are invited to embark on a journey of transformation, a journey that at one and the same time is personal, ecclesial, and missionary. "Mission, then, is much more than the work we do; in itself it becomes a means of ongoing transformation of our own lives," writes theological educator Madge Karecki. She suggests,

> Mission leads us into a more profound sharing in the paschal mystery of Christ. It makes possible a kenotic participation in this mystery of the humility of God made visible in Jesus the Christ as we allow ourselves to be broken and poured out for others in the service of mission. This kind of spirituality, which is not for the faint-hearted, can be embraced only through the work of the Holy Spirit.[160]

As the Arusha Call pointed to the path of discipleship, it began with the awareness that we are "moving in the Spirit." Participation of this movement is what creates the kind of leadership that is needed in church and world today. We are not short of examples of self-centred and destructive leadership. Without the inward transformation that we experience on the path of discipleship, we will not be equipped to offer the very different kind of leadership needed to transform the world.

Questions for Reflection

What kind of leadership do you see when power and wealth are the drivers?

How do servant leaders differ from the usual kind of leaders?

Can you give some examples of women and men, in the past or present, who have proved to be servant leaders?

---

160. Madge Karecki, "A Missiological Reflection on 'Together towards Life: Mission and Evangelism in Changing Landscapes," *International Bulletin of Missionary Research* 38:4 (October 2014), 191–92, at 192.

10. BREAKING DOWN WALLS

We are called to break down walls and seek justice with people who are dispossessed and displaced from their lands – including migrants, refugees, and asylum seekers – and to resist new frontiers and borders that separate and kill (Isaiah 58:6–8).

Migration Today

As delegates from every part of the world gathered at the Conference on World Mission and Evangelism in Arusha, one common concern that soon emerged was the movement of people. In many different contexts, the impact of migration represents a major, often highly controversial, challenge. The 21st century has been called "the age of migration."[161] More people are on the move in the world today than ever before. A September 2019 United Nations report notes that, globally, there are 272 million international migrants, an increase of 51 million since 2010.[162] More disturbingly, UNHCR reported that in the year 2018, "almost 70.8 million individuals were forcibly displaced worldwide as a result of persecution, conflict, violence, or human rights violations."[163] Today, about 3.5 percent of the world's population are migrants, compared to 2.8 percent in 2000. While the percentage may seem small, it represents a lot of people. In fact, if all migrants in the world were to come together to constitute a country, theirs would be the world's fifth most populous.

This is not an entirely new phenomenon. Migration is as old as human history. In every age, individuals and communities have taken the decision to move from one place to another. Many countries today have a population made up of the descendants of migrants who have come from elsewhere at an earlier time in history.[164] Modern communications and transportation have

---

161. See Stephen Castles and Mark Miller, *The Age of Migration: International Population Movements in the Modern World*, 4th edition (Basingstoke: Palgrave MacMillan, 2009).

162. *International Migrant Stock 2019* (New York: United Nations Department of Economic and Social Affairs, 2019), 1.

163. *Global Trends: Forced Displacement in 2018* (New York: UNCHR, 2018), 1.

164. See further Gemma Tulud Cruz, "Migration," in Ross et al., *Ecumenical Missiology*, 340–52, at 340–41.

accelerated the pace, but migration has been a perennial reality of human history. Nonetheless, the modern period has seen an intensification of the movement of people. New possibilities for travel and communication have enabled Europeans to migrate to other continents like never before. The same transport networks enabled migration in the opposite direction, as people from the global South have moved in unprecedented numbers to Europe and North America. Some have been forced to migrate through the slave trade or by catastrophic circumstances in their countries of origin. Others have sought social and economic opportunity on their own initiative. Often the underlying reasons for migration are complex and multi-faceted.

The late 20th and early 21st centuries have seen a growing variety of forms of migration, and immigration has become an increasingly potent political issue in many different contexts. Several European and Asian countries have operated a permit system to allow temporary contract workers to live and work for periods of time without being accorded any citizenship rights. The oil-rich countries of the Gulf have depended for their prosperity on migrant workers from south and southeast Asia who live and work on a temporary basis under closely controlled conditions. The closer integration of the international economy through the effects of globalization has intensified the movement of workers. For some this can represent a welcome new opportunity, but there is also a darker side. As Gemma Tulud Cruz observes,

> the end of the twentieth century saw the increase of clandestine or unauthorised movements of people, particularly unskilled workers, refugees and asylum seekers, a phenomenon which took on unprecedented proportions in the 21st century, not only in volume but also in the often tragic nature of these movements, as destination countries instituted more stringent and more restrictive immigration policies.[165]

A recent WCC report recognized, "To the privileged few, migration may be a 'good experience,' but to most migrants, the realities involve hardships: being uprooted, detained, trafficked or even dying on the journey."[166] These difficulties are greatly compounded by a tendency to "other" migrants, looking on them as a threat to be treated with hostility. In so far as we share such an attitude, we become part of the problem with regard to migration.

---

165. Tulud Cruz, "Migration," 340; see further Gemma Tulud Cruz, *Toward a Theology of Migration: Social Justice and Religious Experience* (New York: Palgrave Macmillan, 2014).

166. *The "Other" Is My Neighbour: Developing an Ecumenical Response to Migration* (Geneva: WCC Publications, 2013), 37.

As the WCC report explains,

> "Othering" of migrants happens when we emphasize difference negatively over and above valuing commonalities or mutuality positively. "Othering" or stereotyping is a process in which mental, psychological and physical fences are constructed to keep out what and whoever appears to be "strange(r)" and as not meeting the requirements or nature of the "in-group." In a search for clear-cut identities, "othering" excludes, inferiorizes and very often hurts and violates those who are not admitted to the "in-group" and into the dominant players' culture(s) and discourses. As such, "othering" can pave the way toward racist attitudes and practices.[167]

These dynamics of "othering" and exclusion were powerfully evoked at the Arusha conference by Agnes Aboum, moderator of the WCC central committee, in her opening address: "We are … concerned about the changing global, regional, and national contexts that are increasingly volatile and uncertain. Indeed, challenges facing the global human community have increased: for example, dislocation and displacement of communities due to conflicts and climate change; growing inequality between a few super rich and millions of poor people; growing populism, nationalism, individualism, xenophobia, and racism."[168] Fundamental questions about human dignity find focus in contemporary approaches to migration.

Breaking Down Walls

The Arusha Call's reference to "breaking down walls" is perhaps its most directly political point, given that several countries around the world are engaged in building walls or other forms of barrier specifically to address a perceived threat from international migrants. Most conspicuously, a key plank in Donald Trump's presidential campaign was his pledge to build a "great, great wall" on the Mexican-American border. He justified his plan by alleging that "[Mexico] are sending people that have lots of problems, and they are bringing those problems to us. They are bringing drugs, and bringing crime, and their rapists."[169] The new President referred to border protection three times during his short inauguration speech. It became clear

---

167. Ibid., 48.

168. Agnes Aboum, "Welcome by the Moderator", in Jukko and Keum, eds., *Moving in the Spirit*, 44–45.

169. Adam Gabbatt, "Donald Trump's Tirade on Mexico's 'Drugs and Rapists' Outrages US Latinos," *The Guardian*, 16 June 2015.

that a nation largely composed of immigrants would now take a hostile view of future aspiring immigrants, even those seeking asylum from violence and insecurity in their countries of origin.

This direction of travel stands clearly in contrast to the view of others, strangers, and immigrants that meets us in the Bible. Thirty-six times in the Hebrew Bible, God's people are commanded to care for the foreigner and the stranger in their land. For example, Deuteronomy 10:19 states, "So you too must befriend the alien, for you were once aliens yourselves in the land of Egypt." Jesus commanded his disciples, "But I say to you, Love your enemies and pray for those who persecute you" (Matthew 5:44). At a time when prejudice, hatred, racism, misogyny, and xenophobia are returning to the mainstream and being validated by those in power, the onus is on disciples of Christ to show that they look on "others" in a very different way.

True Christian faith, far from being a rallying point for hostility toward "others," fosters a radical openness. The new centre found in Jesus Christ "opens the self up, makes it capable and willing to give itself for others and to receive others in itself."[170] As nations and peoples are discipled, they express themselves in the kind of self-giving love in which Christ found his identity and purpose and in which our world may find true hope today. The way of Christ tells us that "trust, defencelessness, and vulnerability are in themselves, despite all appearances, finally more productive and protective than all stratagems for aggression or defence, attack or retaliation, self-assertion or self-protection." Following Christ means being willing "to lead risky, unprotected, costly lives, open to others and committed to self-expenditure on their behalf."[171] Martin Robra has offered a timely reminder of lessons learned from the WCC's "Theology of Life" programme from 1994 to 1998: "Only if they begin to build together a new web of relationships that sustains and nurtures life through common practices of solidarity can people start to engage each other, address the differences between them, and make themselves vulnerable and accessible to others."[172]

---

170. Miroslav Volf, *Exclusion and Embrace: A Theological Exploration of Identity, Otherness and Reconciliation* (Nashville: Abingdon Press, 1996), 71.

171. Alan E. Lewis, *Between Cross and Resurrection: A Theology of Holy Saturday* (Grand Rapids: Eerdmans, 2001), 321, 454.

172. Martin Robra, "Moving in the Spirit: Called to Transforming Discipleship," *International Review of Mission* 105:2 (2016), 243–56, at 251.

Seeking Justice

Such principles clearly set the Christian at odds with the mood of suspicion and xenophobia that prevails in many societies today. Yet the biblical mandate is unambiguous. Christine Pohl, after an extensive review of biblical texts on the alien and hospitality, points out, "The biblical focus on responsibility to resident aliens suggests that a concern for the physical, social and spiritual well-being of migrants and refugees should not be peripheral to Christian life, mission and witness; instead, it should be central."[173] Whether an advocacy role is popular or not, the churches cannot evade it. This may involve costly solidarity with migrants who are mistreated as well as a comprehensive effort to justly address the wider issues raised by today's migratory movements. As the WCC report on migration affirms,

> The realm of God is a vision of a just and united world. The challenge of prophesy and of Jesus' teaching is to liberate and equip Christians to have the courage to work for alternative community, to work for peace and justice, which is to address the causes which uproot people . . . There is no peace without justice or full justice without peace. (Amos 5:24) Our faith compels us to struggle for justice and peace for all; to work for a world where economic, political and social institutions serve people rather than the other way around.[174]

The Arusha Call summons us to this kind of conversion when it draws attention to migrants, refugees, and asylum-seekers. It pointedly calls us to seek justice not *for* but *with* people who are dispossessed and displaced from their lands. Only when we are alongside migrants in welcome and solidarity will we discover the motivation to seek justice and bring transformation to systems that oppress and enslave.

Resisting New Frontiers and Borders

This involves a decidedly political standpoint and one that will run counter to the populist and xenophobic trends that hold sway in many contexts around the world today. As new frontiers and borders are erected as an expression of hostility to migrants, Christians are called to resist. In this they are motivated not only by the biblical vision of justice but also by their experience of the life of the church. The WCC migration report affirms, "As Christians, we affirm

---

173. Christine D. Pohl, "Biblical Issues in Mission and Migration," *Missiology: An International Review* 31:1 (January 2003), 3–15, at 9.

174. *The "Other" Is My Neighbour*, 3.

that the church, the communion of believers, is one through the redemptive work of Christ (Galatians 3:28). Therefore, those who are baptized are joined together as brothers and sisters. We acknowledge that no part of the body can be rejected and no part can claim to be the most important."[175] Such conviction provides a fundamental orientation when it comes to migrants, refugees, and asylum-seekers: "The 'other' is not just tolerated in the kingdom of God, but has an active role to play and a unique contribution to make."[176]

It is also relevant to remember that the church is a pilgrim community. We are all invited to understand ourselves as "sojourners and pilgrims" (1 Peter 2:11). Such an orientation has clear implications for the way we see migrants:

> A church in pilgrimage is . . . aware of fellow travellers who have an equal right to finding shelter, justice, job opportunities, participation rights, access to places of worship, education, residence and contextual identity. It points toward "an active partnership with God in speaking truth to powers, confronting and transforming unjust, inhuman, discriminatory ideologies, cultures and realities, so that the world may be what God always wanted it to be."[177]

Among those on the move are the refugees uprooted by the conflicts that have afflicted many countries in recent times. Despite the widespread resentment against immigrants from the South and the barriers put in their path, it seems safe to predict that South-to-North migration will continue to occur on a massive scale for the foreseeable future. So long as many of the migrants are people of profound and adventurous Christian faith, the potential of this vast movement to contribute to worldwide missionary engagement is enormous. "Mission in the context of migration arising from globalization," suggests Tulud Cruz, "has also changed the face of the missionary from white, western or European to a Christian person of colour from the global South."[178] This is what *Together towards Life* has in mind when it points out that "today we are facing a radically changing ecclesial landscape described as 'world Christianity' where the majority of Christians either are living or have their origins in the

---

175. *Ibid.,* 11.

176. *Ibid.,* 13.

177. *The "Other" Is My Neighbour,* 21, quoting *Global Platform for Theological Reflection 2010: Unity and Mission Today: Voices from the Margins, Bucharest, Romania, 4–10 October 2010,* 13.

178. Tulud Cruz, "Migration," 348.

global South and East. Migration has become a worldwide, multi-directional phenomenon which is reshaping the Christian landscape."[179]

In a major study of this phenomenon, Jehu Hanciles argues that immigrant churches potentially have a missionary function, not only because they represent the most effective instruments through which immigrants can affect the wider society, but also because they model religious commitment, apply the message of the gospel directly to daily exigencies, and comprise communities that interact on a daily basis with other marginalized segments of society.[180] In the perspective of mission from the margins, there is nothing surprising about mission being led by a despised and abused section of the human community.

Resistance takes the form not only of political advocacy and action for justice but also of a recognition that, when it comes to migration, God's economy is very different from that which prevails in the political mainstream. As *Together towards Life* expresses it, "God's hospitality calls us to move beyond binary notions of culturally dominant groups as hosts and migrant and minority peoples as guests. Instead, in God's hospitality, God is host and we are all invited by the Spirit to participate with humility and mutuality in God's mission."[181] Disciples of Christ resist new frontiers and borders because they have discovered a very different way of relating to the phenomenon of migration.

Questions for Reflection

Why are many people today leaving their homes to become migrants?

Why is there so much hostility toward those moving to a new place?

Have you met any people who are migrants, refugees, or asylum seekers? How has meeting them affected you?

---

179. *Together towards Life,* §5.

180. Hanciles, *Beyond Christendom,* 277–78; cited in Tulud Cruz, "Migration," 349.

181. *Together towards Life,* §71.

11. THE WAY OF THE CROSS

We are called to follow the way of the cross,
which challenges elitism, privilege, and personal
and structural power (Luke 9:23).

The Way of the Cross

It is evident that the prevailing values of today's world are, in many respects, antithetical to the values of the gospel of Christ. Those who follow Christ therefore need to be prepared to swim against the tide and to voice a prophetic critique. They are not likely to win any popularity contests. It will be a costly discipleship. To set this discipleship in its proper context, however, it is important to remember that Christian discipleship is not primarily about adopting a political position, protesting against injustice or advocating certain ethical standpoints – even if it may in due course lead to such commitments. Nor is discipleship primarily a matter of adopting a belief structure or becoming a member of an institution – even if such developments may in due course be entailed. Christian discipleship is first of all personal – a matter of a transforming encounter with Jesus Christ, the risen Lord, in the power of the Spirit. This encounter takes the form of a call to take up the cross and follow Jesus. "And Jesus said to all: 'If anyone would come after me, let him deny himself and take up his cross daily and follow me'" (Luke 9:23). The utter self-giving that we see when Christ died on the cross is to be the theme tune of our lives too.

Rowan Williams begins his recent study of the Christian life by observing that "discipleship … is a state of being. Discipleship is about how we live; not just the decisions we make, not just the things we believe, but a state of being."[182] *Together towards Life* states the matter in spiritual terms: "Life in the Holy Spirit is the essence of mission, the core of why we do what we do and how we live our lives."[183] The *Cape Town Commitment* concludes with the affirmation, "Biblical mission demands that those who claim Christ's name should be like him, by taking up their cross, denying themselves, and following him in the paths of humility, love, integrity, generosity, and servanthood. To fail in discipleship and disciple-making, is to fail at the most basic level

---

182. Rowan Williams, *Being Disciples: Essentials of the Christian Life* (London: SPCK, 2016), 1.

183. *Together towards Life,* §3.

of our mission."[184] To be a disciple is, first and foremost, a personal matter. It is about an inward encounter with Christ, the formation of Christ-like character, and the embarking on a way of life that corresponds with the path that Jesus followed.

The Arusha conference was alert to the reality that the rejection and suffering represented by the cross is not a merely theoretical matter. Today, in many parts of the world, especially where Christians are a minority presence, authentic evangelism is indeed a costly commitment, as was the case for the early church under the Roman empire. To defy the imperial dictate that every citizen should declare the Emperor as Lord was a supreme act of evangelical commitment. They knew that it could cost them their lives. By refusing to worship the emperor and the empire, the early church exemplified costly discipleship.

As "The Arusha Conference Report" observes, "Today, empires are striking back in new forms, with their own dictatorial requirements of allegiance to mammon, market, consumerism, militarism, sexism, racism, fascism, and fundamentalism. Bearing the cross implies a willingness to confront the logic of the empire and to lay down our lives for the sake of Christ and the gospel." As Dietrich Bonhoeffer wrote: 'when Christ calls a man [or woman] he bids him [her] to come and die.'"[185]

On its final day, the Arusha conference was reminded by His Holiness Mor Ignatius Aphrem II, Patriarch of Antioch and All the East and Supreme Head of the Universal Syrian Orthodox Church, that this martyr's path is a reality for many disciples today:

> … Christians face rejection in their societies. Severe forms of rejection lead to persecution, where hatred is expressed in the forms of violence and the desire to exterminate. Christians throughout the world are victims of persecution; large numbers of Christian communities in all continents face persecution on a daily basis. It comes in different forms and varies greatly: it can be the lack of freedom of religious beliefs, or actively killing innocent children or families while they are peacefully praying or worshipping the Lord.[186]

The conference met with full awareness of such sobering realities. One of its preparatory documents observed that

---

184. *Cape Town Commitment*, Conclusion.

185. "The Arusha Conference Report," 17.

186. His Holiness Mor Ignatius Aphrem II, "Embracing the Cross Today in the Context of the Middle East," in Jukko and Keum, eds., *Moving in the Spirit*, 148–51, at 149–50.

in today's world, martyrdom continues to be an expression of joyous evangelism, as was reflected poignantly in the widely publicized execution of 21 Coptic Orthodox Christians on the Mediterranean coast near Sirte in Libya by ISIS terrorists in 2015. These Egyptian migrant workers died with prayers to Jesus on their lips, teaching us all the joy of costly discipleship. This is a supreme expression of "joyous evangelism" which is kenotic and cross-bearing.[187]

The suffering and death of our contemporary fellow Christians in contexts such as Syria and Libya are powerful reminders that the call to take up the cross is not just a figure of speech but rather a costly reality.

Challenging Elitism and Privilege

"The Arusha Conference Report" affirmed,

Discipleship is a costly vocation. It is a matter of being broken and poured out for others in the service of mission. Where our ministries have become self-seeking, consumerist, and prosperity oriented, we need to hear anew Christ's call to take up our cross and follow him (Luke 9:23). We have far too often presented Christian vocation in ways that avoided disturbing the status quo and interpreted it as good behaviour of humility, resilience, servanthood, sacrifice, gentleness, cordial interpersonal relationships, and so on. Furthermore, it is risky because it involves confronting, exposing, and resisting such hostile forces as the rise of populist politics, the revival of racism and xenophobia, corporate greed, inequality and injustice in the global economy, renewed danger of nuclear warfare, and threats to the integrity of the earth itself. Behind all of these forces are powerful vested interests that will not take kindly to being challenged. Transforming discipleship is not going to be cheap. It requires us to step out of our comfort zones.[188]

By drawing attention to elitism and privilege, the Arusha Call reminds us that the life of discipleship cannot be lived in the abstract. It can, and must, be lived in the concrete reality of the world in which disciples are placed. Pope Francis has urged, "No one can demand that religion should be relegated to the inner sanctum of personal life, without influence on societal and national life, without concern for the soundness of civil institutions, without a right to offer an opinion on events affecting society."[189] As we live a different way

---

187. "Being Disciples Means Sharing Good News," 231.

188. "The Arusha Conference Report," 17.

189. Pope Francis, *Evangelii Gaudium*, §183.

of life and, implicitly or explicitly, offer a prophetic critique of the norms and values of the society around us, there is a price to be paid.

A Different Kind of Power

The Arusha Call provokes us to think about power, both the power that we exercise as individuals and the structures of power of which we are a part. The way of the cross represents a challenge to and subversion of prevailing forms of power. Rather than being seduced by self-centred forms of power, disciples are called to discover that God's power "is made perfect in weakness" (2 Cor. 2:9). As His Holiness Mor Ignatius Aphrem II told the conference,

> In today's world, people seem to be focused on themselves; it is easy to be drawn to self-centrism and egoism. However, nurturing one's basic spiritual needs should not lead to narcissism or self-centralism. Nurturing one's basic spiritual needs is a healthy way to seek spiritual growth "until all of us come to the unity of the faith and of the knowledge of the Son of God, to maturity, to the measure of the full stature of Christ." (Eph. 4:13) We are then called disciples of Christ.[190]

In a divided world, a religious community can be tempted to assert its own power. The Arusha Call points us in a very different direction, as noted in "The Arusha Conference Report":

> In our neighbourhoods and globally, there are examples of peaceful co-existence but also of interreligious intolerance, bigotry, violence, and persecution. God has given us the ministry of reconciliation (2 Corinthians 5:18) . . . Bringing hope might imply relief efforts, involvement in advocacy and development work, and actively supporting various forms of interreligious encounters, particularly among younger generations. Moreover, the conference sought answers to the question of what is a faithful response when our neighbours of another religion become targets of hatred and violence? How are we called, as disciples of Christ, to embrace the cross for their sake?[191]

---

190. His Holiness Mor Ignatius Aphrem II, "Embracing the Cross Today," 149.

191. "The Arusha Conference Report," 18.

Called to Follow

The conference was reminded of the definition of missionary discipleship given by *Mission and Evangelism: An Ecumenical Affirmation* in 1982: "The self-emptying of the servant who lived among the people, sharing in their hopes and sufferings, giving his life on the cross for all humanity – this was Christ's way of proclaiming the good news, and as disciples we are summoned to follow the same way."[192] The Arusha Call sustains this radical challenge to a consumerist society. The path of discipleship is one that involves renouncing the priority of our own interests in favour of radical self-giving.

One of the Arusha conference's preparatory documents made an important connection:

> *Kenosis* is integrally related to necrosis. Self-denial and cross-bearing are two essential aspects of authentic discipleship (Mark 8:34). These are not about certain acts of self-mortification or curbing of certain desires of the body through some rigorous self-discipline. As German theologian Dietrich Bonhoeffer reminds us, it is about being other-centric, being oriented towards those who are poor and marginalized. It is when we are in solidarity with those who are suffering and when we share the pain of love for the other that we meaningfully empty ourselves and bear the cross. In this sense, discipleship is a costly affair. It stands in contradiction to the cheap grace that is experienced in ministries of evangelism that are self-seeking, consumerist and prosperity-oriented, as there is hardly any cost involved here. When we offer solidarity to others in their struggle for justice, we also share both their pain and joy (hope for a better tomorrow) through the gospel.[193]

In making this call to give ourselves radically for others, the Arusha Call echoes the insights of ecumenical and mission leaders of earlier generations. Commenting on the biblical text "He that findeth his life shall lose it; and he that loseth his life for my sake shall find it," J. H. Oldham unfolded a paradox: "The human heart is so constituted that its fullness comes of spending. When we serve we rule. When we give we have. When we surrender ourselves we are victors. We are most ourselves when we lose sight of ourselves."[194]

Our calling, as Bishop Festo Kivingere often said to younger leaders within the East African Revival, is to be "broken bread and poured out wine."[195]

---

192. *Mission and Evangelism: An Ecumenical Affirmation* (Geneva: WCC, 1983), §28.

193. "Being Disciples Means Sharing Good News," 230–31.

194. Matthew 10:39; J.H. Oldham, *A Devotional Diary* (London: SCM, 1925), Second Month, Day 19.

195. Festo Kivingere, cited in Jørgensen, *Equipping for Service*, 40.

A lifetime in the missionary movement allowed John Taylor to conclude, "Every opening of one's whole self towards another, every taking upon oneself the burden and the gift of another, contributes a little to that quiet tide which is flowing back and forth, carrying us with it into the very being of God, sweeping us back with God into the life of the world."[196]

Questions for Reflection

Can you give examples of the kind of power that is challenged by the way of the cross?

What do you think are the main characteristics of the way of the cross?

What might the way of the cross mean for you personally at this time?

---

196. Cited in David Wood, *Poet, Priest and Prophet: Bishop John V. Taylor* (London: CTBI, 2002), 210.

12. PEOPLE OF HOPE

We are called to live in the light of the resurrection, which offers hope-filled possibilities for transformation.

Resurrection People

A focus on taking up the cross, on self-denial, suffering, and death, takes us to the heart of what it means to follow Jesus. Yet we have missed something vital if it appears that death has the last word. For in the case of Jesus, death proved to be the prelude to resurrection. So it is also in the experience of those who follow him. In the Christian proclamation, death and resurrection belong inseparably together. Therefore, when the Arusha Call summons us to take the way of the cross, this pathway must lead, in the end, to resurrection.

Christians are resurrection people: "If Christ has not been raised, then our proclamation has been in vain and your faith has been in vain" (1 Cor. 15:14). This, of course, has a bearing on how we think about death. The supposed finality of death is undermined as the resurrection of Christ opens up a horizon of hope to all who trust in him. Given our human mortality, this is something that can never be underestimated.

Yet the experience of resurrection hope pertains not only to death but also to life. Death and resurrection are a lived experience here and now, memorably captured by the apostle Paul when he wrote to the Corinthians, "We are afflicted in every way, but not crushed; perplexed, but not driven to despair; persecuted, but not forsaken; struck down, but not destroyed; always carrying in the body the death of Jesus, so that the life of Jesus may also be made visible in our bodies" (2 Cor. 4:8–10). As we have seen, many Christians in today's world are subject to great adversity. Still, the joy and hope of the resurrection define their experience. "No, in all these things," protested Paul, "we are more than conquerors through him who loved us" (Rom. 8:37).

Filled with Hope

Hope is something that comes from God and comes in a very specific form in the resurrection of Christ from the dead. It is when he has reflected at length on the death and resurrection of Jesus that the apostle Paul is able to offer his prayer, "May the God of hope fill you with all joy and peace in believing, so that you may abound in hope by the power of the Holy Spirit" (Romans 15:13). Such hope is not an illusion but is grounded in the realities to which the New Testament bears witness. As Alan Lewis writes, "The day is coming when a Lamb that has been slain, vulnerable and blood-stained, will sit beside the throne, and his triumph will be shared by fellow sufferers who have likewise been abused by injustice, tormented by pain, crushed by sin and terrified by death."[197]

This vision of faith does not entail any blithe optimism that fails to reckon with the harsh realities that are often directly in front of us. This is a deeply realistic form of hope, one that reckons with painful adversities yet remains convinced that these do not have the last word. Whatever may be against us, the resurrection "offers hope-filled possibilities of transformation." Such hope supplies staying power when we meet with complex and intractable situations of injustice that can often appear to leave us defeated. Faith can provoke a sense of urgency while at the same time allowing us to recognize the penultimate character of the contemporary struggle and return to the ultimate vision for fresh inspiration and energy whenever this is needed. In this way, Christians can bring a passionate urgency to the great moral challenges of our time while also having the staying power generated by the resurrection hope that frames their faith.

Pope Francis captures what this means in terms of the immediate experience of faith: "I invite all Christians, everywhere, at this very moment, to a renewed personal encounter with Jesus Christ, or at least an openness to letting him encounter them; I ask all of you to do this unfailingly each day . . . Let us not flee from the resurrection of Jesus, let us never give up, come what will."[198] No matter what may occur that would cast us down, as resurrection people our heads are lifted again by the horizon of hope that frames our faith.

<hr>

197. Lewis, *Between Cross and Resurrection*, 65.

198. Pope Francis, *Evangelii Gaudium*, §3.

New Possibilities

The Arusha Call finishes on a note of "hope-filled possibilities." It does not hold back in identifying death-dealing forces that are shaking the foundations of life in our time. Yet, in the end, it offers the conviction that "another world is possible." As Collin Cowan stated, in his sermon at the Arusha conference Sending Service,

> Jesus' calling of his first disciples was set in the context of the forces of empire that tempted him with popularity and pleasure over the principles of obedience and faithfulness to God. Jesus, having resisted the temptations, presented himself to the community as one not easily sold to the scandal of seduction. His call "Come, follow me" is a statement of rejection of the status quo, and a declaration of an alternative. It is an invitation to defy the established order, divesting oneself of all that is known and held dear, to participate in God's work of transformation . . . being ready to go against the grain of culture, to confront power, challenge status quo and exemplify a lifestyle marked by courage to stand up for what is right and commitment to do justice, love mercy, and walk humbly with God (Micah 6:8).[199]

When we enter the realm of love, we enter the realm of new possibilities. Love distinguished the path that Jesus chose, a love that depends not on the attractiveness of the one who is loved but entirely on the grace and power of the one who loves. This is the love that Jesus, at infinite cost to himself, brought to all those who were excluded, those who were on the margins of society, the poor, the sick, the outcast.

The quality of this love was deeply disturbing to the powers that be, upsetting their carefully constructed assumptions that loving was something to be done within very well-defined limits. It was so disturbing, in fact, that very soon Jesus put himself at risk. Forces at large were ready to crush and destroy anyone who set about loving without any limits. Eventually, Jesus was engulfed by these forces and made final proof of the fact that his love went on even to the uttermost. On the cross, he demonstrated that self-interest is not, cannot be, the ultimate motivating force on which the world runs. There is something stronger, something deeper, that alone is the true spring of life – it is the love that refuses to acknowledge any limits and that will go on loving no matter what the cost.

It is this love that took Jesus to his death on the cross but proved too strong for death, and so Jesus rose and lives today to bring this remarkable quality of

---

199. Collin Cowan, "Sermon at the Sending Service," in Jukko, Keum, and Woo, *Called to Transforming Discipleship*, 88–89.

love to our world. When we are embraced by this great love, it becomes the defining reality of our lives too. John says, "Since God loved us so much, we also ought to love one another" (1 John 4:11). It has been said that the only way for a Christian to live is to risk love and hope for resurrection. To love is going to be risky. In fact, it is going to be so risky that it is going to mean death. It meant death for Jesus and it will mean death for us in many different ways. Jesus knew what he was talking about when he spoke of taking up our cross daily. But he also knew that death leads to resurrection. As we suffer the death to which love leads us, our lives fill up with the glory of resurrection.

The glory is there to be received, to be lived. But to reach it we need to go the risky way of Jesus – to risk love and hope for resurrection. Most of us are cautious by nature. We have a strong instinct to look after ourselves and not to expose ourselves unnecessarily. Naturally, we shy away from risking love, from letting the quality of love we meet in Jesus become the theme song of our lives. That is why it is such a radical decision to become a Christian. Gustavo Gutiérrez of Peru put it like this: "To be converted is to know and experience the fact that, contrary to the laws of physics, we can stand straight, according to the Gospel, only when our centre of gravity is outside ourselves."[200] It was only because Jesus found his centre of gravity outside of himself that he was able to give himself for us. Now his love moves us to find our centre of gravity outside ourselves – across the divide – and it is only as we undergo that radical realignment that we discover what it is to be a disciple. The risky way of love means death, but it also means resurrection and no end of new possibilities.

Transformation

To be a disciple is, first and foremost, a personal matter. It is about an inward encounter with Christ, the formation of Christ-like character, and the embarking on a way of life that corresponds with the path that Jesus followed. As this inward transformation takes place, we are, at the same time, shaped so as to become agents of transformation. We are privileged to join in the mission of the triune God, working together towards life, living out the values of the kingdom of God, and engaging in Christ's mission. In a world in which injustice seems almost insuperable, where hatred and racism seem to thrive, where suffering is so widespread and terrifying, our discipleship is costly. We are called to take up our cross and follow Christ. We are called

---

200. Gustavo Gutiérrez, *A Theology of Liberation: History, Politics, and Salvation* (Maryknoll: Orbis, 1973), 205.

to spend our energy and even offer our lives for the transformation that the kingdom promises.

We will look in vain for political solutions to our predicament if we are not willing to embark on the journey of inward transformation that turns us into agents of transformation in the world around us. In Jesus' decisive encounter with Peter he said to him, "You are Simon son of John. You are to be called Cephas" (which is translated Peter [from the word for rock])" (John 1:42). In the ancient near east, a name carried power. It was not just what someone happened to be called. It was an indication of their character. It summed up what they were all about. In the biblical tradition, when God gave someone a new name, it meant that their life would be taking on new character and going in a new direction.

From everything that we know about Peter, he was anything but a rock. He was an impulsive, volatile, unreliable character. But to be a disciple is to be on a journey of transformation. In Peter's case, this means he was going to become a rock-like person. Such entirely new possibility comes into play when someone "comes to see" what Jesus is all about. The power of a new life is at work and entirely new possibilities open up. We can never underestimate the transformation that begins when someone "comes to see" and makes their decision to follow Jesus.

It would be naïve to underestimate the cost that will be involved in following Jesus in a world driven by values so often opposed to those found in the reign of God. Yet the last word belongs not with the risk or the pain that discipleship may entail. It was the theologian of costly discipleship, Dietrich Bonhoeffer, who perhaps articulated most clearly the Christological reality that death leads to resurrection, that self-denial leads to fulfillment, that you lose your life in order to find it:

> And if we answer the call to discipleship, where will it lead us? What decisions and partings will it demand? To answer this question we shall have to go to him, for only he knows the answer. Only Jesus Christ, who bids us follow him, knows the journey's end. But we do know that it will be a road of boundless mercy. Discipleship means joy.[201]

This joy, however, is found not by escaping from the challenges posed by harsh current realities but rather by embracing them. This faith is a transformative faith. The great missiologist David Bosch asserted,

---

201. Dietrich Bonhoeffer, *The Cost of Discipleship*, 2nd ed. (New York: Macmillan, 1959), 41.

> We know that evil, injustice, hatred, estrangement, prejudice and fear will never entirely disappear from the face of the earth before the kingdoms of this world are finally consummated in the Kingdom of God. But the moment we allow this harsh reality to paralyse us and sabotage our efforts, we can no longer pray the Lord's Prayer – "thy Kingdom come, thy will be done, *on earth* as in heaven." To offer that prayer implies believing that Christians make a difference to this world . . . the community of those who are enjoying a foretaste of perfection – should get involved in God's mission of transforming the world.[202]

This transforming power has more recently been evoked by Pope Francis when he stated,

> However dark things are, goodness always re-emerges and spreads. Each day in our world beauty is born anew, it rises transformed through the storms of history. Values always tend to reappear under new guises, and human beings have arisen time after time from situations that seemed doomed. Such is the power of the resurrection, and all who evangelize are instruments of that power.[203]

Today's world is crying out for this kind of renewing power. The challenges in front of us, locally and globally, are such that something extraordinary is needed to meet them. The Arusha Call proposes that it is in hearing anew Jesus' invitation to discipleship that we will discover the vision, energy, and courage needed to meet the crisis of our times. This proposal is an invitation made to everyone. No one is excluded. It is a costly choice, framed in terms of taking up the cross.

Yet life itself is at stake. It is time to be decisive. The Holy Spirit is moving. Christ's death and resurrection can take effect in our lives through the power of the Spirit. The path of discipleship beckons. Inward transformation will form us into the kind of people who can have a transforming effect in the world around us. As we become such disciples, we become agents of the renewal of God's mission in our time.

---

202. David J. Bosch, "The Kingdom of God and the Kingdoms of This World," *Journal of Theology for Southern Africa* 29 (December 1979), 3–13, at 12–13.

203. Pope Francis, *Evangelii Gaudium*, §276.

Questions for Reflection

What difference does the resurrection of Christ make to the way we live our lives?

What kind of transformation can you imagine in view of Christ's resurrection?

In your own context, what "hope-filled possibilities" can you identify?

CONCLUSION:
TOGETHER AS MISSIONARY DISCIPLES

Time to Come Together

The meaning of discipleship is a question with wide currency in world Christianity today. The special contribution of "The Arusha Call to Discipleship" lies, to a great extent, in its ecumenical character. It was prepared, debated, affirmed, adopted, and promoted by an extraordinarily wide spectrum of global Christianity. It is the product of a process that brought together Orthodox, Protestant, Catholic, Anglican, independent, evangelical, and Pentecostal expressions of Christianity. As committed and thoughtful people within these different streams have grappled with the question of the meaning of mission in the early 21st century, they have found themselves gravitating in the same direction. This direction takes them back to the call to discipleship, issued by Jesus, with which the story of Christianity began. It impels them to explore what it means to respond to that call in relation to the profound and pressing challenges presented by the 21st-century context, global and local.

This convergence in regard to the meaning of mission is not something to be taken for granted. For the Protestant churches, the 20th century wrote a story of divergence as far as missiological understanding is concerned. Even the Edinburgh 1910 World Missionary Conference, celebrated as the starting point of the modern ecumenical movement, could meet only on the basis that discussions would be restricted to the practicalities of mission and avoid divisive ecclesial and doctrinal questions.[204] Moreover, at that time meaningful cooperation with the Catholic and Orthodox churches was a distant dream, and the newly emergent Pentecostal movement was not even considered. To make matters worse, the 20th century saw the Protestant missionary movement splitting into two camps, often described as "ecumenical" and "evangelical." This division has run deep and been definitive for identity, association, theology, and practice in many different contexts around the world.[205]

The WCC's 2005 Conference on World Mission and Evangelism in Athens and the Edinburgh 2010 World Missionary Conference signalled that, in the 21st century, division and fragmentation might be giving way to a new

---

204. See Brian Stanley, *The World Missionary Conference, Edinburgh 1910* (Grand Rapids: Eerdmans, 2009), 37–41.

205. See further Kenneth R. Ross, "The Arusha Call: Signal of Missiological Convergence?" *International Review of Mission* 107:2 (December 2018), 443–57.

convergence. This found documentary expression in the 2012 WCC mission affirmation, *Together towards Life*. Jooseop Keum, its editor, explained that "the new affirmation is an ecumenical conviction. It articulates diverse understandings of mission of different traditions and contexts and comprehensively addresses them through ecumenical convergence."[206]

Together towards Life could potentially be criticized on the grounds that it simply set differing understandings of mission alongside one another rather than enabling them to inform one another. Familiar ecumenical concern with issues of justice appear in early sections, such as those on "Transformative Spirituality" and "Mission from the Margins," while familiar evangelical concerns with proclamation and conversion appear in the final major section on "Good News for All: the Call to Evangelize."

Nonetheless, signs of convergence are plain to see in *Together towards Life*, and these are further highlighted when the WCC document is compared with two almost contemporaneous mission texts issued by two other major constituencies in world Christianity: the *Cape Town Commitment* of the Lausanne Movement in 2010, and Pope Francis' *Evangelii Gaudium* in 2013. John Armstrong remarked that "when you put TTL and CTC together with *Evangelii Gaudium* (EG), you might be inclined to become downright giddy about the future of missional-ecumenism in the church."[207]

Arusha Call as Convergence Text

"The Arusha Call to Discipleship" takes this movement of convergence a stage further. It picks up the pneumatological orientation of *Together towards Life*, which, among other things, has opened up a fresh dimension that has proved to be unifying. The strains of *Together towards Life* are evident in the Arusha Call's opening affirmation: "We joyfully celebrated the life-giving movement of the Spirit of God in our time". It goes on to state that the conference approached its task through "Bible study, common prayer and worship". The deliberations and conclusion of the conference are unquestionably grounded in faith, worship, and spirituality. The opening affirmation, while it begins with pneumatology, is also robustly trinitarian and Christological: "We were encouraged to be witnesses to the reign of God that has come to

206. "CWME: From Athens to Arusha – Director's Report" in Jukko and Keum, eds., *Moving in the Spirit*, 73–87, at 77.

207. John H. Armstrong, "The Church in the Contemporary Ecumenical-Missional Moment: Together towards Life in Dialogue with The Cape Town Commitment and Evangelii Gaudium," *International Review of Mission* 104:2 (2015), 232–41, at 234.

us through the life, crucifixion, and resurrection of our Lord Jesus Christ."[208] Affirming the deep foundations on which shared faith rests offers a centre of unity that draws different traditions together.

A renewed focus on discipleship offers an inviting point of convergence. As it takes courage in face of a disturbing and challenging global context, the Call affirms that "the Holy Spirit continues to move at this time, and urgently calls us as Christian communities to respond with personal and communal conversion, and a transforming discipleship."[209] Personal conversion is a characteristic evangelical concern, conversion being one of the four pillars of the "Evangelical Quadrilateral."[210] In balancing this with communal conversion and the agenda of transformation, the Call takes account at the same time of characteristic ecumenical concerns. It goes on, in the first section of the 12-part Call, to state, "We are called by our baptism to transforming discipleship: a Christ-connected way of life in a world where many face despair, rejection, loneliness, and worthlessness."[211] This speaks to the characteristically evangelical concern that there is a life of faith, a spiritual life, at the heart of Christianity that is definitive and requires to be nourished. At the same time, the orientation of discipleship to the whole of life speaks to characteristically ecumenical concerns about contextuality, social issues, and our contemporary crisis.

In rather a bold move, the Call further introduces discipleship by referring to a characteristic feature of Orthodox theology:

> In what the church's early theologians called "theosis" or deification, we share God's grace by sharing God's mission. This journey of discipleship leads us to share and live out God's love in Jesus Christ by seeking justice and peace in ways that are different from the world. Thus, we are responding to Jesus' call to follow him from the margins of our world.[212]

By giving a new twist to the understanding of *theosis*, viewing it as a matter of sharing in God's mission, it opens up this concept to evangelical constituents, who would not normally find it in their vocabulary or theological apparatus. Following this, the Arusha Call skilfully interweaves evangelical

---

208. "The Arusha Call to Discipleship," 2.

209. Ibid.

210. See further David W. Bebbington, *Evangelicalism in Modern Britain: A History from the 1730s to the 1980s* (London: Routledge, 1988).

211. "The Arusha Call to Discipleship," 2.

212. Ibid., 2.

and ecumenical language – integrating "sharing and living out God's love" with "seeking justice and peace"; and integrating "Jesus' call to follow him" with the question of the margins.[213]

Such integration is further evident in the Call's recognition that we are called to proclaim the gospel "in a violent world where many are sacrificed to the idols of death (Jeremiah 32:35) and where many have not yet heard the gospel."[214] Concern for those who have not heard the good news of Christ has been a defining concern of the Lausanne Movement. Here, it is given unequivocal recognition, but alongside an equal concern for the many who "are sacrificed to the idols of death" – opening up wide-ranging possibilities for prophetic exposure of destructive forces at work in the world.

One area that has often polarized ecumenicals and evangelicals is the question of how to relate to other religions. The responsibility to witness to the uniqueness of Christ has often been uppermost in evangelical thinking, leading to an emphasis on evangelism. The responsibility to work for peace and reconciliation has often been uppermost in ecumenical thinking, leading to an emphasis on dialogue. This has often appeared to be an either/or divergence. The Arusha Call, however, is attentive to both sides: "We are called to be faithful witnesses of God's transforming love in dialogue with people of other faiths in a world where the politicization of religious identities often causes conflict."[215] From either side, people will find their concerns being recognized here. This is more, however, than a matter of diplomatic niceties. The Call offers a fresh integration of apparently contrasting concerns, so that witness and dialogue are held in a creative tension that is alert to the challenges of our contemporary context while setting these against the open horizon of the transforming love of God.

As it sounds the call to discipleship, the document strikes notes that point to a common agenda in countering forces opposed to the way of Christ. "We are called to be formed as servant leaders who demonstrate the way of Christ in a world that privileges power, wealth, and the culture of money... We are called to follow the way of the cross, which challenges elitism, privilege, personal and structural power."[216] The Call puts differences in emphasis into perspective when it clarifies what is at stake in answering the call to discipleship – never more so than in the last of the 12 parts: "We are called to

---

213. Ibid., 3.

214. Ibid.

215. Ibid.

216. Ibid.

live in the light of the resurrection, which offers hope-filled possibilities for transformation."[217]

Unfinished Business

To make any definitive judgment would be premature, but indications are that "The Arusha Call to Discipleship" may come to be recognized as a milestone on the road to convergence in the understanding of the meaning of mission within the world Christian community. Already significant is the fact that delegates could come from the varied constituencies found within world Christianity and, together, form a detailed and impassioned statement of their common missionary calling in the contemporary situation. Their coming together in Arusha, their sharing in prayer and table fellowship, their common struggle with the biblical calling in relation to current social and political trends, their achievement of consensus in what is required to be said as a call to church and world – all of this indicates that polarization is giving way to convergence. Close examination of the way the Arusha Call has been framed and composed demonstrates an intentionality behind this convergence. The text reflects a deliberate listening to one another and a determined attempt to reflect one another's concerns and speak one another's language.

The movement of convergence is plain to see, and the Arusha Call may well come to be recognized as having taken it to a new stage. Nonetheless, the Call also reveals the limitations and shortcomings of this movement. It has achieved a great deal in bringing together constituencies that had been at odds and finding that they can forge common understanding in mission thinking. At the same time, this has been achieved, to a considerable extent, by a tacit agreement to set aside points on which it is harder to reach agreement or consensus. On issues such as the understanding of sexual identity, for example, different constituencies clearly bring deep concerns. These can be voiced on occasion, but it tends to be a matter of speaking *alongside* each other rather than *to* each other. This is already a beginning but one that makes apparent how much remains to be done in terms of deepening the dialogue and strengthening mutual understanding.

The Arusha Call, while remarkable for how much it can say, at the same time reveals, by its silence in certain areas, the extent of unfinished business left for the movement of convergence. Nonetheless, even while acknowledging significant remaining challenges, we can conclude that the Arusha Call is a signal of missiological convergence. Whereas the prevailing pattern during

---

217. Ibid.

the second half of the 20th century was one of divergence in regard to understanding the meaning of mission, the first two decades of the 21st century have seen a movement of convergence. "The Arusha Call to Discipleship" demonstrates how far that movement has come.

Needed Today: Missionary Disciples

We need greater historical distance to fully take account of the convergence in missiological thinking evident in the first two decades of the 21st century. One of the drivers, however, is already all too evident. The global crisis in this period has become so severe that disunity and divergence in relation to Christian mission begin to look like a luxury we cannot afford.

The Arusha Call does not spare us when it comes to elaborating the various dimensions of our contemporary crisis: despair, rejection, loneliness, and worthlessness; the false god of the market system; violent and death-dealing forces; lack of justice and dignity; fake news and manipulative media; a ruthless human-centred exploitation of the environment for consumerism and greed; marginalization and exclusion; politicization of religious identities stoking conflict; domination of the culture of money; new frontiers and borders that separate and kill; and concentration of power and privilege in the hands of elites. As the Arusha delegates surveyed the world of the early 21st century, this is what they saw. Faced by such a deadly array of destructive forces, they discovered afresh the urgent importance of their unity in Christ and of their calling to bear witness to the gospel of life.

This led them to listen afresh to Christ's call to discipleship. "Follow me," said Jesus to his first disciples. It was in responding to this invitation that they found themselves becoming active in mission. Two millennia later, after the meaning of Christian mission has been defined and expressed in many different ways and in a moment of acute crisis for the world and its people, the global Christian community is once again finding its identity and calling in the summons of Jesus. "Whoever serves me must follow me, and where I am, there will my servant be also" (John 12:26). When we are "moved by the Spirit," this is the direction we will take. As this path proved costly for Jesus, so it will be for those who follow. This death, however, leads to resurrection. It is through our commitment to walk this path of discipleship that the mission of God takes effect in the world, ministering the life and hope that are so greatly needed today.

This is a call to transforming discipleship.

SELECT BIBLIOGRAPHY

Allen, Roland. *Missionary Methods: St Paul's or Ours? A Study of the Church in the Four Provinces.* London: Robert Scott, 1912.

Anderson, Allan. *An Introduction to Pentecostalism.* Cambridge: Cambridge University Press, 2004.

Appleby, R. Scott. *The Ambivalence of the Sacred: Religion, Violence and Reconciliation.* Lanham and Oxford: Rowman and Littlefield, 2000.

Armstrong, John H. "The Church in the Contemporary Ecumenical-Missional Moment: *Together towards Life* in Dialogue with *The Cape Town Commitment* and *Evangelii Gaudium.*" *International Review of Mission* 104:2 (November 2015), 232–41.

Bebbington, David W. *Evangelicalism in Modern Britain: A History from the 1730s to the 1980s.* London: Routledge, 1988.

Bevans, Stephen. "Prophetic Dialogue and Intercultural Mission." In *Intercultural Mission*, ed. Lazar T. Stanislaus and Martin Üffing, 201–14. Sankt Augustin, Germany: Steyler Missionswissenschaft Intitut and Delhi: ISPCK, 2015.

Bevans, Stephen. "Transforming Discipleship and the Future of Mission: Missiological Reflections after the Arusha World Mission Conference." *International Review of Mission* 107:2 (December 2018), 362–77.

Bevans, Stephen B., and Roger P. Schroeder. *Constants in Context: A Theology of Mission for Today.* Maryknoll, NY: Orbis, 2004.

Bonhoeffer, Dietrich. *The Cost of Discipleship.* 2nd edition. New York: Macmillan, 1959.

Bosch, David. "The Kingdom of God and the Kingdoms of This World." *Journal of Theology for Southern Africa* 29 (1979), 3–13.

Bosch, David. *Transforming Mission: Paradigm Shifts in Theology of Mission.* New York: Orbis, 1991.

The Cape Town Commitment: A Confession of Faith and a Call to Action. Lausanne Movement, 2011.

Castles, Stephen, and Mark Miller. *The Age of Migration: International Population Movements in the Modern World.* 4th edition. Basingstoke: Palgrave MacMillan, 2009.

The Church: Towards a Common Vision. Faith and Order Paper No. 214. Geneva: WCC, 2013.

Climate Change and Poverty: Report of the Special Rapporteur on Extreme Poverty and Human Rights. New York: United Nations, 2019.

Collier, Jane, and Rafael Esteban. *From Complicity to Encounter: The Church and the Culture of Economism.* Harrisburg: Trinity Press, 1998.

Come and See: A Theological Invitation to the Pilgrimage of Justice and Peace. Faith and Order Paper No. 224. Geneva: WCC, 2019.

Conner, Benjamin. "Discipleship." In *Ecumenical Missiology: Changing Landscapes and New Conceptions of Mission*, ed. Kenneth R. Ross, Jooseop Keum, Kyriaki Avtzi and Roderick R. Hewitt, 246–58. Oxford: Regnum / Geneva: WCC Publications, 2016.

Conradie, Ernst M. *Christianity and Earthkeeping: In Search of an Inspiring Vision.* Stellenbosch: Sun Press, 2011.

Conradie, Ernst M. "Environment." In *Ecumenical Missiology: Changing Landscapes and New Conceptions of Mission*, ed. Kenneth R. Ross, Jooseop Keum, Kyriaki Avtzi, and Roderick R. Hewitt, 320–30. Oxford: Regnum / Geneva: WCC Publications, 2016.

Early, Tracy. *Simply Sharing – A Personal Survey of How Well the Ecumenical Movement Shares its Resources.* Geneva: WCC Publications, 1980.

Francis, Pope. *Evangelii Gaudium: Apostolic Exhortation to the Bishops, Clergy, Consecrated Persons and the Lay Faithful on the Proclamation of the Gospel in Today's World.* Rome: Vatican Press, 2013.

Francis, Pope. *Laudato Si': On Care for Our Common Home.* Rome: Vatican Press, 2015.

Gill, David, ed. *Gathered for Life: Official Report VI Assembly World Council of Churches Vancouver, Canada 24 July – 10 August 1983.* Geneva: WCC Publications, 1983.

Gittins, Anthony J. *The Way of Discipleship: Women, Men and Today's Call to Mission.* Collegeville: Liturgical Press, 2016.

Gnanakan, Ken. "To Proclaim the Good News of the Kingdom," In *Mission in the 21st Century: Exploring the Five Marks of Global Mission*, ed. Andrew Walls and Cathy Ross, 3–10. London: Darton, Longman and Todd, 2008.

Granberg-Michaelson, Wesley. *Future Faith: Ten Challenges Re-Shaping Christianity in the 21st Century.* Philadelphia: Fortress Press, 2018.

Granberg-Michaelson, Wesley. *Leadership From Inside Out: Spirituality and Organizational Change.* New York: Crossroad, 2004.

Gutiérrez, Gustavo. *A Theology of Liberation: History, Politics, and Salvation.* Maryknoll, NY: Orbis, 1973.

Hanciles, Jehu J. *Beyond Christendom: Globalization, African Migration and the Transformation of the West.* Maryknoll, NY: Orbis, 2008.

Hyde-Riley, Merlyn. "Following Jesus: Becoming Disciples, Mark 6:1–13." In *Called to Transforming Discipleship: Devotions from the World Council of Churches Conference on World Mission and Evangelism*, ed. Risto Jukko,

Jooseop Keum and (Kay) Kyeong-Ah Woo, 7–14. Geneva: WCC Publications, 2019.

Jenkins, Philip. *The Next Christendom: The Coming of Global Christianity*. Oxford: Oxford University Press, 2002.

Johnson, Todd M., and Kenneth R. Ross, eds. *Atlas of Global Christianity*. Edinburgh: Edinburgh University Press, 2009.

Jørgensen, Knud. *Equipping for Service: Christian Leadership in Church and Society*. Oxford: Regnum, 2012.

Jukko, Risto, ed. *Conference on World Mission and Evangelism, 2018. Complete Digital Edition of the Arusha Report.* https://www.oikoumene.org/en/resources/publications/DigitalEdition_ArushaReport_ALL.pdf.

Jukko, Risto, and Jooseop Keum, eds. *Moving in the Spirit: Report of the World Council of Churches Conference on World Mission and Evangelism, 8–13 March 2018, Arusha, Tanzania*. Geneva: WCC Publications, 2019.

Jukko, Risto, Jooseop Keum, and (Kay) Kyeong-Ah Woo, eds. *Called to Transforming Discipleship: Devotions from the World Council of Churches Conference on World Mission and Evangelism*. Geneva: WCC Publications, 2019.

Karecki, Madge. "A Missiological Reflection on 'Together towards Life: Mission and Evangelism in Changing Landscapes.'" *International Bulletin of Missionary Research* 38:4 (October 2014), 191–92.

Keum, Jooseop Keum, ed. *Together towards Life: Mission and Evangelism in Changing Landscapes*. Geneva: WCC Publications, 2013.

Kim, Dongsung. "Partnership and Resource-Sharing." In *Ecumenical Missiology: Changing Landscapes and New Conceptions of Mission*, ed. Kenneth R. Ross, Jooseop Keum, Kyriaki Avtzi, and Roderick R. Hewitt, 259–70. Oxford: Regnum / Geneva: WCC Publications, 2016.

Kim, Kirsteen. "Mission after the Arusha Conference on World Mission and Evangelism, 2018." *International Review of Mission* 107:2 (December 2018), 413–27.

Kim, Kirsteen, and Andrew Anderson, eds., *Edinburgh 2010: Mission Today and Tomorrow*. Oxford: Regnum, 2011.

Kraemer, Hendrik. *The Christian Message in a Non-Christian World*. London: Edinburgh House Press, 1938.

Küng, Hans. *Christianity, Essence, History, Future*. London: Continuum, 1996.

Lanchester, John. "Brexit Blues." *London Review of Books* 38:15 (28 July 2016), 3–6.

Lewis, Alan E. *Between Cross and Resurrection: A Theology of Holy Saturday*. Grand Rapids: Eerdmans, 2001.

Manchala, Deenabandhu. "Margins." In *Ecumenical Missiology: Changing Landscapes and New Conceptions of Mission*, ed. Kenneth R. Ross, Jooseop Keum, Kyriaki Avtzi and Roderick R. Hewitt, 309–19. Oxford: Regnum / Geneva: WCC Publications, 2016.

Matthey, Jacques, ed. *Come Holy Spirit, Heal and Reconcile! Called in Christ to Be Reconciling and Healing Communities – Report of the WCC Conference on World Mission and Evangelism, Athens, Greece, May 9–16, 2005.* Geneva: WCC Publications, 2008.

Mission and Evangelism: An Ecumenical Affirmation. Geneva: WCC, 1983.

Newbigin, Lesslie. *Is Christ Divided? A Plea for Christian Unity in a Revolutionary Age.* Grand Rapids: Eerdmans, 1961.

Newbigin, Lesslie. *The Good Shepherd: Meditations on Christian Ministry in Today's World.* Grand Rapids: Eerdmans, 1977.

Newbigin, Lesslie. *The Open Secret: Sketches for a Missionary Theology.* Grand Rapids: Eerdmans, 1978.

Newbigin, Lesslie. *The Other Side of 1984: Questions for the Churches.* Geneva: WCC Publications, 1983.

Noort, Gerrit, Kyriaki Avtzi, and Stefan Paas, eds. *Sharing Good News: Handbook on Evangelism in Europe.* Geneva: WCC Publications, 2017.

Oldham, J. H. *A Devotional Diary.* London: SCM, 1925.

Orwell, George. *Nineteen Eighty-Four.* London: Secker and Warburg, 1949.

The "Other" Is My Neighbour: Developing an Ecumenical Response to Migration. Geneva: WCC, 2013.

Piketty, Thomas. *Capital in the Twenty-first Century.* Boston: Harvard University Press, 2014.

Pohl, Christine D. "Biblical Issues in Mission and Migration." *Missiology: An International Review* 31:1 (January 2003), 3–15.

Rajkumar, Peniel. "Other Faiths." In *Ecumenical Missiology: Changing Landscapes and New Conceptions of Mission*, ed. Kenneth R. Ross, Jooseop Keum, Kyriaki Avtzi and Roderick R. Hewitt, 218–34. Oxford: Regnum / Geneva: WCC Publications, 2016.

Robinson, Gnana, ed. *Sharing and Living – A Study on the Ecumenical Sharing of Resources in India.* Madurai, India: Nepolean Press, 1983.

Robra, Martin. "*Moving in the Spirit*: Called to Transforming Discipleship." *International Review of Mission* 105:2 (November 2016), 243–56.

Ross, Kenneth R. "The Arusha Call: Signal of Missiological Convergence?" *International Review of Mission* 107:2 (December 2018), 443–57.

Ross, Kenneth R. "Tracing Changing Landscapes and New Conceptions of Mission." In *Ecumenical Missiology: Changing Landscapes and New Conceptions of Mission*, ed. Kenneth R. Ross, Jooseop Keum, Kyriaki Avtzi and

Roderick R. Hewitt, 5–146. Oxford: Regnum / Geneva: WCC Publications, 2016.

Ross, Kenneth R., and Wonsuk Ma. "Conclusion: Spirituality as the Beating Heart of Mission." In *Mission Spirituality and Authentic Discipleship*, ed. Wonsuk Ma and Kenneth R. Ross, 225–33. Oxford: Regnum, 2013.

Roy, Arundhati. *The Ordinary Person's Guide to Empire*. London: Harper Perennial, 2004.

Sanneh, Lamin. *Disciples of All Nations: Pillars of World Christianity*. New York: Oxford University Press, 2008.

Sanneh, Lamin. *Translating the Message: The Missionary Impact on Culture*. Maryknoll, NY: Orbis, 1989.

Stanley, Brian. *The World Missionary Conference, Edinburgh 1910*. Grand Rapids: Eerdmans, 2009.

Tulud Cruz, Gemma. "Migration." In *Ecumenical Missiology: Changing Landscapes and New Conceptions of Mission*, ed. Kenneth R. Ross, Jooseop Keum, Kyriaki Avtzi, and Roderick R. Hewitt, 340–52. Oxford: Regnum / Geneva: WCC Publications, 2016.

Vallely, Paul. *Pope Francis: Untying the Knots*. London: Bloomsbury, 2013.

Volf, Miroslav. *Exclusion and Embrace: A Theological Exploration of Identity, Otherness and Reconciliation*. Nashville: Abingdon Press, 1996.

Währisch-Oblau, Claudia. "Evangelism." In *Ecumenical Missiology: Changing Landscapes and New Conceptions of Mission*, ed. Kenneth R. Ross, Jooseop Keum, Kyriaki Avtzi, and Roderick R. Hewitt, 151–66. Oxford: Regnum / Geneva: WCC Publications, 2016.

Wallis, Jim. *God's Politics: Why the American Right Gets It Wrong and the Left Doesn't Get It*. Oxford: Lion, 2005.

Walls, Andrew F. "Mission and Migration: The Diaspora Factor in Christian History." *Journal of African Christian Thought* 5:2 (December 2002), 3–11.

Webber, Robert. *Ancient-Future Faith*. Grand Rapids: Baker Books, 1999.

Whitmore, William. "The Branch Is Linked to the Vine: Personal Discipleship and the *Missio Dei*." *International Review of Mission* 107:2 (December 2018), 472–82.

Wickeri, Philip L. "Mission from the Margins: The *Missio Dei* in the Crisis of World Christianity." *International Review of Mission* 93 (April 2004), 182–98.

Williams, Rowan. *Being Disciples: Essentials of the Christian Life*. London: SPCK, 2016.

Wilson, Frederick R., ed. *The San Antonio Report: Your Will Be Done: Mission in Christ's Way*. Geneva: WCC Publications, 1990.

Wood, David. *Poet, Priest and Prophet: Bishop John V. Taylor*. London: CTBI, 2002.

World Alliance of Reformed Churches. *Letter from Accra*. Geneva: World Alliance of Reformed Churches, 2004.

WCC Publications is the book publishing programme of the World Council of Churches. It facilitates global Christianity's "alternative voice" and enhances the larger visibility and cultural presence of the ecumenical movement.

The WCC publishes works that specifically engage religious and social issues confronting world Christianity, inform and encourage the ecumenical movement, and provide resources for research on ecumenical history and theology.

To order WCC books:

Europe and worldwide

Email orders to: orders@wcc-coe.org

https://www.oikoumene.org

Globethics.net is an ethics network of teachers and institutions based in Geneva, with an international Board of Foundation and with ECOSOC status with the United Nations. Our vision is to embed ethics in higher education. In order to ensure access to knowledge resources in applied ethics, Globethics.net has developed four resources:

Globethics.net Library & Globethics.net Publications

The leading global digital library on ethics and a publishing house open to all the authors interested in applied ethics.

Globethics.net Academy & Globethics.net Network

Online and offline courses and training for all on ethics and a global network of experts and institutions including a Pool of experts and a Consortium

www.globethics.net

WCC Publications 2018-2020

A comprehensive list of WCC Publications can be found on the Resources section of https://www.oikoumene.org

Donald Norwood, *Pilgrimage of Faith: The Journey of the WCC*, 2018, ISBN: 978-2-8254-1710-2

Carlos Sentado and Manuel Quintero Perez, *A Legacy of Passionate Ecumenism*, 2018, ISBN: 978-2-8254-1711-9

Susan Durber and Fernando Enns (Eds.), *Walking Together: Reflections on the Ecumenical Pilgrimage of Justice and Peace*, 2018, ISBN: 978-2-8254-1712-6

J. Michael West and Gunnar Mägi (Eds.), *Your Word Is Truth: The Bible in Ten Christian Traditions*, 2018, ISBN: 978-2-8254-1714-0

J. Michael West and Gunnar Mägi (Eds.), *Your Word Is Truth: The Bible in Ten Christian Traditions*, eBook edition, 2018, ISBN: 978-2-8254-1715-7

Treatment Adherence and Faith Healing in the Context of HIV and AIDS in Africa (EHAIA), 2018, ISBN: 978-2-8254-1716-4

Treatment Adherence and Faith Healing in the Context of HIV and AIDS in Africa (EHAIA), Kiswahili edition, 2018, ISBN: 978-2-8254-1717-1

Treatment Adherence and Faith Healing in the Context of HIV and AIDS in Africa (EHAIA), French, 2018, ISBN: 978-2-8254-1718-8

Positive Masculinities and Femininities: Handbook for Adolescents and Young People in Faith Communities in Nigeria, English edition, 2018, ISBN: 978-2-8254-1719-5

Translating the Word, Transforming the World: An Ecumenical Reader, 2018 ISBN: 978-2-8254-1712-6

Amélé Adamavi-Aho Ekué, Pamela D. Couture, and Samuel George (Eds.), *For Those Who Wish to Dream: Emerging Theologians on Mission and Evangelism,* 2019, ISBN: 978-2-8254-1724-9

Risto Jukko and Jooseop Keum (Eds.), *Moving in the Spirit: Report of the WCC Conference on World Mission and Evangelism,* 2019, ISBN: 978-2-8254-1721-8

Risto Jukko (Ed.), *Moving in the Spirit: Report of the WCC Conference on World Mission and Evangelism,* Complete Digital Edition, 2019, ISBN: 978-2-8254-1722-5

Risto Jukko, Jooseop Keum and (Kay) Kyeong-Ah Woo (Eds.), *Called to Transforming Discipleship: Devotions from the WCC Conference on World Mission and Evangelism,* 2019, ISBN: 978-2-8254-1723-2

Come and See: A Theological Invitation to the Pilgrimage of Justice and Peace (Faith & Order Paper 224), 2019, ISBN: 978-2-8254-1725-6

Susan Durber and Fernando Enns (Eds.), *Walking Together: Reflections on the Ecumenical Pilgrimage of Justice and Peace,* Ebook edition, 2019, ISBN: 978-2-8254-1726-3

United and Uniting Churches: Two Messages (Faith and Order Paper 225), 2019, ISBN: 978-2-8254-1727-0

Pontifical Council for Interreligious Dialogue and the World Council of Churches, *Education for Peace in a Multi-Religious World: A Christian Perspective,* 2019, ISBN: 978-2-8254-1728-7

Moral Discernment in the Churches, Spanish edition, 2019, ISBN: 978-2-8254-1700-3

Moral Discernment in the Churches, German edition, 2019, ISBN: 978-2-8254-1729-4

Treatment Adherence and Faith Healing in the Context of HIV and AIDS in Africa (EHAIA), Kinwaranda Version, 2019, ISBN: 978-2-8254-1701-0

They Showed Us Unusual Kindness: Resources for the Week of Prayer for Christian Unity 2020 (F&O Paper 226), 2019, ISBN: 978-2-8254-1704-1

Minutes of the Faith and Order Commission Meeting (Nanjing, June 2019, Faith & Order Paper 227), 2019, ISBN: 978-2-8254-1705-8

Fulata Lusungu Moyo, *Healing Together: A Facilitator's Resource for Ecumenical Faith and Community Community-Based Counselling* (EHAIA), 2019, ISBN: 978-2-8254-1706-5

Jürgen Moltmann, *Hope in These Troubled Times,* 2019, ISBN: 978-2-8254-1713-3

Mwai Mokoka, *Health-Promoting Churches: Reflections on Health and Healing for Churches on Commemorative World Health Days,* 2020, ISBN: 978-2-8254-1708-9

Mwai Mokoka, *Health-Promoting Churches: Reflections on Health and Healing for Churches on Commemorative World Health Days,* Spanish edition, 2020, ISBN: 978-2-8254-1709-6

Ecumenical International Youth Day, 2020: Young People and Mental Health, 2020, ISBN: 978-2-8254-1730-0

Climate Justice with and for Children and Youth in Churches: Get Informed, Get Inspired, Take Action, 2020, ISBN: 978-2-8254-1731-7

The Light of Peace: The Churches and the Korean Peninsula, 2020, ISBN: 978-2-8254-1732-4

Healing the World: Bible Studies for the Pandemic Era, 2020, ISBN: 978-2-8254-1733-1

The Light of Peace: Churches in Solidarity with the Korean Peninsula, 2020, ISBN: 978-2-8254-1734-8

Pontifical Council for Interreligious Dialogue and the World Council of Churches, Serving a Wounded World in Interreligious Solidarity: A Christian call to reflection and action during COVID-19 and beyond, 2020, ISBN: 978-2-8254-1737-9

Globethics.net Publications

The list below is only a selection of our publications. To view the full collection, please visit our website.

All free products are provided free of charge and can be downloaded in PDF form from the Globethics.net library and at www.globethics.net/publications. Bulk print copies can be ordered from *publications@globethics.net* at special rates from the Global South.

Paid products not provided free of charge are indicated*.

The Director of the different Series of Globethics.net Publications
Prof. Dr. Obiora Ike, Executive Director of Globethics.net in Geneva and Professor of Ethics at the Godfrey Okoye University Enugu/Nigeria.

Contact for manuscripts and suggestions: publications@globethics.net

Global Series

Obiora Ike, Andrea Grieder and Ignace Haaz (Eds.), *Poetry and Ethics: Inventing Possibilities in Which We Are Moved to Action and How We Live Together,* 271pp. 2018, ISBN: 978–2–88931–242–9

Christoph Stückelberger / Pavan Duggal (Eds.), *Cyber Ethics 4.0: Serving Humanity with Values,* 503pp. 2018, ISBN: 978–2–88931–264-1

Texts Series

Water Ethics: Principles and Guidelines, 2019, 41pp. ISBN: 978–2–88931-313-6

Éthique de l'eau: Principes et lignes directrices, 2019, 34pp. ISBN: 978-2-88931-325-9

Ética del agua: Principios y directrices, 2020, 48pp. ISBN: 978-2-88931-343-3

Theses Series

A. Halil Thahir, *Ijtihād Maqāṣidi: The Interconnected Maṣlaḥah-Based Reconstruction of Islamic Laws,* 2019, 200pp. ISBN: 978-2-88931-220-7

Tibor Héjj, *Human Dignity in Managing Employees. A performative approach, based on the Catholic Social Teaching (CST)*, 2019, 320pp. ISBN: 978-2-88931-280-1

Sabina Kavutha Mutisya, *The Experience of Being a Divorced or Separated Single Mother: A Phenomenological Study*, 2019, 168pp. ISBN: 978-2-88931-274-0

Florence Muia, *Sustainable Peacebuilding Strategies. Sustainable Peacebuilding Operations in Nakuru County, Kenya: Contribution to the Catholic Justice and Peace Commission (CJPC)*, 2020, 195pp. ISBN: 978-2-88931-331-0

Mary Rose-Claret Ogbuehi, *The Struggle for Women Empowerment Through Education*, 2020, 410pp. ISBN: 978-2-88931-363-1

Focus Series

John M. Itty, *Search for Non-Violent and People-Centric Development*, 2017, 317pp. ISBN: 978–2–88931–185–9

Florian Josef Hoffmann, *Reichtum der Welt—für Alle Durch Wohlstand zur Freiheit*, 2017, 122pp. ISBN: 978–2–88931–187–3

Cristina Calvo / Humberto Shikiya / Deivit Montealegre (eds.), *Ética y economía la relación dañada*, 2017, 377pp. ISBN: 978–2–88931–200–9

Maryann Ijeoma Egbujor, *The Relevance of Journalism Education in Kenya for Professional Identity and Ethical Standards*, 2018, 141pp. ISBN: 978–2–88931233–7

Christoph, Stückelberger, *Globalance. Ethics Handbook for a Balanced World Post-Covid*, 2020, 608pp. ISBN: 978-2-88931-368-6

Praxis Series

Oscar Brenifier, *Day After Day 365 Aphorisms*, 2019, 395pp. ISBN: 978-2-88931-272-6

Christoph Stückelberger, *365 Way-Markers*, 2019, 416pp. ISBN: 978-2-88931-282-5 (Available in English and German).

Benoît Girardin / Evelyne Fiechter-Widemann (Eds.), *Blue Ethics: Ethical Perspectives on Sustainable, Fair Water Resources Use and Management,* 2019, 265pp. ISBN: 978-2-88931-308-2

Benoît Girardin / Evelyne Fiechter-Widemann (Eds.), *Éthique de l'eau: Pour un usage et une gestion justes et durables des ressources en eau,* 2020, 309pp. ISBN: 978-2-88931-337-2

Didier Ostermann, *Le rôle de l'Église maronite dans la construction du Liban : 1500 ans d'histoire, du Ve au XXe siècle,* 2020, 142pp. ISBN: 978-2-88931-365-5

Agape Series

崔万田 Cui Wantian, *爱+经济学 Agape Economics,* 2020, 420pp. ISBN: 978-2-88931-349-5

Cui Wantian, Christoph Stückelberger, *The Better Sinner: A Practical Guide on Corruption,* 2020, 37pp. ISBN: 978-2-88931-339-6 (Available also in Chinese).

Anh Tho Andres Kammler, *FaithInvest: Impactful Cooperation. Report of the International Conference Geneva 2020,* 2020, 70pp. ISBN: 978-2-88931-357-0

China Christian Series

Spirituality 4.0 at the Workplace and FaithInvest - Building Bridges, 2019, 107pp. ISBN: 978-2-88931-304-4

海茵兹・吕格尔 / 克里斯多夫・芝格里斯特 (Christoph Sigrist/ Heinz Rüegger) *Diaconia: An Introduction. Theological Foundation of Christian Service,* 2019, 433pp. ISBN: 978-2-88931-302-0

Faith-Based Entrepreneurs Stronger Together. Report of the International Conference Geneva 2018, 2018, 86pp. ISBN: 978-2-88931-258-0

China Ethics Series

Liu Baocheng/Chandni Patel, *Overseas Investment of Chinese Enterprises. A Casebook on Corporate Social Responsibility,* forthcoming 2020, ISBN: 978-2-88931-355-6.

Liu Baocheng / Zhang Mengsha, *CSR Report on Chinese Business Overseas Operations,* 2018, 286pp. ISBN: 978-2-88931-250-4

刘宝成（Liu Baocheng）/ 张梦莎（Zhang Mengsha），中国企业"走出去"社会责任研究报告, 2018, 267pp. ISBN: 978-2-88931-248-1

Education Ethics Series

Divya Singh / Christoph Stückelberger (Eds.), *Ethics in Higher Education Values-driven Leaders for the Future,* 2017, 367pp. ISBN: 978–2–88931–165–1

Obiora Ike / Chidiebere Onyia (Eds.), *Ethics in Higher Education, Foundation for Sustainable Development,* 2018, 645pp. ISBN: 978-2-88931-217-7

Obiora Ike / Chidiebere Onyia (Eds.), *Ethics in Higher Education, Religions and Traditions in Nigeria* 2018, 198pp. ISBN: 978-2-88931-219-1

Obiora F. Ike, Justus Mbae, Chidiebere Onyia (Eds.), *Mainstreaming Ethics in Higher Education: Research Ethics in Administration, Finance, Education, Environment and Law Vol. 1,* 2019, 779pp. ISBN: 978-2-88931-300-6

Deivit Montealegre / María Eugenia Barroso (Eds.), *Ethics in Higher Education, a Transversal Dimension: Challenges for Latin America. Ética en educación superior, una dimensión transversal: Desafíos para América Latina,* 2020, 148pp. ISBN: 978-2-88931-359-4

Education Praxis Series*

Tobe Nnamani / Christoph Stückelberger, *Resolving Ethical Dilemmas in Professional and Private Life. 50 Cases from Africa for Teaching and Training,* 2019, 235pp. ISBN: 978-2-88931-315-0

CEC Series

Elizabeta Kitanović / Patrick Roger Schnabel (Eds.), *Religious Diversity in Europe and the Rights of Religious Minorities,* 2019, 131pp. ISBN: 978-2-88931-270-2

Göran Gunner, Pamela Slotte and Elizabeta Kitanović (Eds.), *Human Rights, Religious Freedom and Faces of Faith,* 2019, 282pp. ISBN: 978-2-88931-321-1

CEC Flash Series

Moral and Ethical Issues in Human Genome Editing. A Statement of the CEC Bioethics Thematic Reference Group, 2019, 85pp. ISBN: 978-2-88931-294-8

Philosophy Series

Ignace Haaz, *The Value of Critical Knowledge, Ethics and Education: Philosophical History Bringing Epistemic and Critical Values to Values*, 2019, 234pp. ISBN: 978-2-88931-292-4

Ignace Haaz, *Empathy and Indifference: Philosophical Reflections on Schizophrenia*, 2020, 143pp. ISBN: 978-2-88931-345-7

Copublications & Other

Patrice Meyer-Bisch, Stefania Gandolfi, Greta Balliu (éds.), *L'interdépendance des droits de l'homme au principe de toute gouvernance démocratique. Commentaire de Souveraineté et coopération*, 2019, 324pp. ISBN: 978-2-88931-310-5

Obiora F. Ike, *Applied Ethics to Issues of Development, Culture, Religion and Education*, 2020, 280pp. ISBN: 978-2-88931-335-8

Obiora F. Ike, *Moral and Ethical Leadership, Human Rights and Conflict Resolution – African and Global Contexts*, 2020, 191pp. ISBN: 978-2-88931-333-4

Kenneth R. Ross, *Mission Rediscovered: Transforming Disciples. A Commentary on the Arusha Call to Discipleship*, 2020, 130pp. ISBN: 978-2-88931-369-3

Reports

Managing and Teaching Ethics in Higher Education. Policy, Skills and Resources: Globethics.net International Conference Report 2018, 2019, 206pp. ISBN: 978-2-88931-288-7

This is only selection of our latest publications, to view our full collection please visit:

www.globethics.net/publications

www.ingramcontent.com/pod-product-compliance
Lightning Source LLC
LaVergne TN
LVHW050610200726
843508LV00010B/1802